Small Town

ORDER AND IMAGE
IN THE AMERICAN
Small Town

Edited by

Michael W. Fazio
and
Peggy Whitman Prenshaw

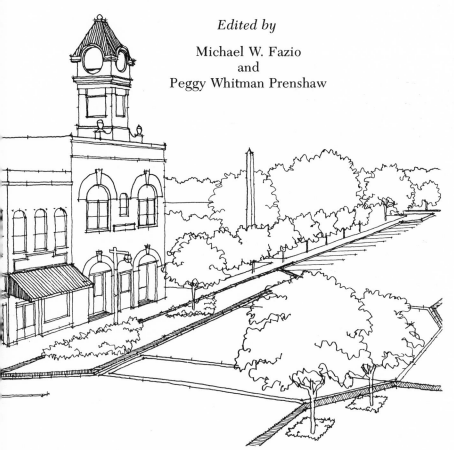

UNIVERSITY PRESS OF MISSISSIPPI
JACKSON

Library of Congress Cataloging in Publication Data

Main entry under title:
Order and image in the American small town.

(Southern quarterly series)
Papers presented at a symposium held at Mississippi
State University, Starkville, Oct. 4–6, 1979.
   1. City and town life—Congresses.   I. Fazio,
Michael W.   II. Prenshaw, Peggy Whitman.   III. Series.
HT107.O73   307.7′6   80–24300
ISBN 0–87805–130–9

Contents

Preface

The papers for this issue of the *Southern Quarterly* were presented at "Chautauqua in Mississippi: Order and Image in the American Small Town," a symposium held on the campus of Mississippi State University, Starkville, October 4–6, 1979. The opening event was the formal dedication of the Center for Small Town Research and Design as a research and service component of the School of Architecture. The final activity, a circuit ride to several Mississippi communities, concluded with a small town celebration, complete with brass band and a picnic on the campus of the Mississippi University for Women in Columbus.

Sponsored by the Mississippi Committee for the Humanities and the School of Architecture at Mississippi State University, this "Chautauqua in Mississippi" was held for the purpose of examining the quality of life in the American small town. The following articles represent part of the symposium's goal, to bring together persons from a wide variety of disciplines for an exchange of ideas about small towns.

Small Town

Introduction:
Order and Image in the American Small Town

The title for this publication was selected carefully. Order and image are powerful words that have various meanings for each of the disciplines represented here: literature, geography, anthropology, landscape architecture, economics, political science and government, architecture, and history. Small town America offers an abundance of order in most Americans' minds, and few images are stronger than the ones which the small town evokes—images as comforting as apple pie and bandstands. These terms, *order* and *image,* seem uniquely appropriate to an investigation and an understanding of the American small town.

Order, both social and physical, derives from a hierarchy within a community that involves economic structure, religious heritage, and racial organization. This is the stuff of William Faulkner's writing. The social order of a small town may appear confusing to an outsider, but it makes perfect sense to those who live within the hierarchy. Because of the scale of small towns, people are seen as wholes, not as parts. Certainly there is prejudice and injustice, but people seem truly to matter as people. Every person experiences something of the lives of everyone else within the social order of a small town.

Physical order originates from the union of topography, architecture, social structure, land values, and political decision making. Physical order is also manifest in the nature of materials, in the special environmental conditions present, and in the response to the natural landscape—in short, in the vernacular. The vernacular response is what gives each small town its unique character, its personality, its image.

The small town image consists of sounds, smells, conversations,

3

patterns, vistas, and emotions. It is a paradoxical truth that we slowly create our small towns in our image, and then they slowly rebuild us in theirs. Image is subtle, yet in determining what we value about small towns, it possesses great power.

To illustrate the power of the small town image, consider some common word pictures of the American town which most natives share: a warm summer evening with a brass band in the courthouse square bandstand playing just off key; a Fourth of July parade down the main street with almost everyone in town watching; a church social in autumn with all day singing and dinner on the ground; a general store which sells nails, bolts, crackers, tobacco, and good fellowship, all of this packed into a tiny building with a dark floor of wood; a tree lined street filled with front porches and neighbors sitting, talking to one another. These are pleasing images that many of us long for.

Such images, of course, invite the charge of blind optimism—perhaps rightfully so. Consider by contrast, then, the following complementary scenes: a bandstand in the courthouse square that is deteriorated, no longer used since the new shopping mall was built on the bypass; the band's passing by on the Fourth of July arousing the crowd only to ask why white faces alone populate the band; the church social, with all-day singing and dinner on the ground, interrupted by a construction crew erecting a new Jitney Jungle grocery directly next door ("You can't stand in the way of progress"); the old general store with a "Closed" sign on the front door, the new K-Mart now selling all the same items in nice clean rows of shelves, replacing former fellowship with a Muzak system; the old tree lined neighborhood street now in the midst of change since the strip development has grown so near that the street is marked for commercial zoning.

My point here is that a number of us possess a subtle schizophrenia concerning the small town image. We love it for its picturesque qualities and its sense of community, but we hate it for its narrowness of thought and its slowness to respond to change. These different perspectives and the issues that arise from them form part of the subject of the following papers.

A small town, like every human community, is characterized by tradition, continuity, and change. A small town's personality would be nothing without its tradition. Sinclair Lewis's stories emphasize the strength of such tradition and its influence on people. Of course, small towns may suffer from a stifling nostalgic tradition which thwarts vitality and vision. On the other hand, nostalgia can be an impetus for growth. For example, Americans are moving to small towns in ever increasing numbers. Many of these Americans are moving in an effort to return home, at least to return to a community like their hometowns. They are seeking a retreat to the order and image of the past, a refuge from urban areas, crime, pollution, and congestion. They are attempting to recover a time that was simpler and less confusing, and the small town seems to be the one place that has maintained the simpler time, in a kind of frozen condition. This is a dangerous misperception, however. Certainly we should value the tradition of the small town—without it such communities would have no real character and no real meaning—but we must consider the small town as a viable present community that has unique current qualities to offer its citizens. It is not a museum of a time when things were easier.

By the same token, we must not consider the small town of the present simply to be a big city waiting to happen. A chief disease of the American small town is an over-emphasis on progress, growth and prosperity. The steam shovel of economic self interest can destroy the vital roots of tradition and the quality of life that makes the small town unique.

Clearly, one cannot have a small town lifestyle if the small town gets big. This ridiculously simple irony is important. We move to small communities to obtain a quality of life that is unique, one which we cannot find in cities or in rural areas. If too many of us make this choice, however, we lose the very qualities we sought. Or, put another way, if a small town's goal is growth, not quality of life, then the small town's lifestyle is doomed.

A small town is a fragile thing. If it decreases in size there are not enough services to sustain the American lifestyle. If it increases in size, the very special qualities of "small" are lost. I believe that the future small town must get tougher and more world-wise to sustain the special qualities necessary for small town living.

What issues will a tougher, better prepared, better organized small town need to address? What happens when the concepts of small town and change come together?

Energy is a topic which has received much attention in recent years. Its impact is beginning to be felt in small towns in the price of gasoline, but the major impact of energy is still coming. The small town of the future must begin planning today for this significant change. The successful town will be one which has centralization of energy sources and reduction of individual energy sources. These sources will utilize a number of natural energy systems.

The planning commission of the future will reward compression in land area instead of expansion in planning and development. There will be a general tightening up of land area so that travel distances will be decreased. This will mean an increased emphasis on a single central place for human services, and the existing downtown will be the logical place for these services.

In the successful small town of the future, the nature of strip development found along many of the bypasses or along the entries into small communities will change significantly. A decrease in emphasis on automobile shopping will have a significant impact on these present growth areas. The exact nature of this strip development will be decided by those responsible for planning for change in tomorrow's small town.

If the trickling of our population from urban areas to small towns continues and grows, the successful small town will structure growth. There will be a significant emphasis on growth planning. The unsuccessful small town of the future will continue its present planning policies.

Shifts in living preferences will lead to a seller's market for the small town, but small town residents should guard against a tendency to gloat over their relative good fortune. The population changes could bring urban problems to the countryside. In fact, as Anne S. Denman notes in a November 1978 editorial in *Small Town,* significant population shifts hold dangers for both the abandoned and the preferred places.

In the course of significant change the successful small town of the future must maintain the kind of climate and tradition that will nurture its people, that will produce and sustain such writers, scientists, painters, politicians, sports heroes, and beauty queens as William Faulkner, Sinclair Lewis, Thomas Edison, Andrew Wyeth, Jackson Pollack, Jimmy Carter, Archie Manning and Cheryl Prewitt.

The papers in this collection analyze and celebrate the American small town—its order and its image. They represent an exchange of ideas concerning the tradition, the continuity, and the change in the American small town. They extend the timeless search for the elusive qualities that create a sense of community.

James F. Barker

Order, Investment and Appropriation

DONLYN LYNDON

Traveling across the United States, or even ruminating over its map, brings forcefully to mind two central and rudimentary observations about small towns—how very many of them there are and what an incredible expenditure of energy and optimism they represent. To stake out a place, name it, parcel its land and provide access to those parcels, develop its institutions, erect its buildings and cultivate the landscape, then establish and re-establish its government every few years—all this is a great enterprise. It involves expenditures of time, physical and emotional energy, and rational endeavor that are astounding. And, of course, it has been done over and over again, often under the most trying circumstances and in the most unlikely locations. We cannot but be humbled, I think, if we place these efforts against our own.

We would do ill—we have done ill—to neglect the resource that these places afford us. But wasted resources are, alas, common to our nation; whole areas of cities lie fallow or poisoned. If we are to affirm that we can make good in the world, can provide as well as destroy those environments that nurture our collective being, then the habits and attitudes of the city as well as those of the small town must be addressed. We need to build an awareness of the cultivated and built environment, of the care that has been invested in it, and of the consequences of unthinking acts upon it. Commitment to acting upon that awareness is an even more difficult corollary. The development of awareness and responsibility—of an ethos—is not an overnight project, nor even very often the consequence of an extended project. Understanding is fragile; responsible commitment is even more so.

One is tempted to suppose that in small towns it should be easier to

8

develop a viable community consciousness. The very attributes of smallness seem promising: fewer people to convince, more personal accountability to recognizable peers, a set of physical characteristics and problems that seem easier to comprehend, perceptible boundaries, and consequences that become evident in the immediate vicinity. But this assumption might be invalid; the judgment of peers may often be tyrannous, the physical characteristics may be deceiving and the most difficult forces at work may be outside the local view, so far removed from control that they induce paralysis. Nevertheless, the framework for community consciousness that is provided by the physical structure of a small town offers a special sort of hope and is, I think, important to pursue.

As the setting for actions repeated day after day, the places in which we live become channels for thought, props in the stories we tell ourselves about who we are, with whom we live, and why. The places in which we live become indices for our own internal narrative, reminding us of many things, shielding us from others. The place may be rich with suggestions, even overwhelming, or it may be bleak. In either case it will afford us a certain set of incidents each day, a particular set of signposts, a physical context with specific opportunities and limits—hard facts that bond ideas together.

What might we seek of a place that would provide support for the development of community consciousness, a place that would provide the chance for its residents to be reminded of their collective heritage and to recognize responsibility for its nurture? Three things at least: distinctness, evidence of the social context, and opportunities for appropriation.

Distinctness

We would seek to know that we were in a distinct place, one that could be recognized and distinguished from its neighbors. Small towns have the great advantage that their elements are few, their extent limited. Main Street begins and ends; the public buildings claim their special position in the town; the institutions are evident and identifiable; and the variations in the town's structure, types of housing stock, industrial and commercial uses of land all take place in a small compass. In a few minutes you can traverse a cross section of the place and its diversity is readily accessible to view. Being few, and readily grasped, its various elements make a recognizable pattern, a place often of distinction. Like features on a face, they form a configuration that can be held in the mind.

Evidence of a Social Context

It has become a truism that our towns reflect our social selves, a culture or heritage that informs us of the values of the past. We often see two responses to this: a group committed to selective editing of the past, with a very pointed, revisionist view of history, or, on the other hand, total abandonment to the view that every action taken reflects our society, so no judgments are to be made. Our view of the small town as social evidence should be more pointed. Precisely what is of interest in the small town of our dreams is the tension between an implicit idealism and a messy democratic picture of ourselves. Generally, the small town embodies the phenomena of elements of imposed order coexisting with signs of inhabitation, with the adjustments, accommodations and ornery inventiveness of those who have lived in the place.

The order of most small towns, I contend, exists in fragments, lodged in concrete, imageable bits, often in conflict with each other. An idyllic tree-shaded, house-lined street dissolves into a Main Street of distinct length, with facade walls forming a definite public meeting place of an altogether different character. This, in turn, is interrupted by a public or religious building that claims dominion over its surroundings, as though perched on a hill commanding the valley. Each building type, by its form and by its siting, implies an image of order. The coexistence, even competition, of these building types is evidence of the complex social compact under which we live. Within each of these projected visions of order there are variations of intention, and they have been imagined quite differently. Their fragmentary, overlapping quality is like us—a society that has become what it is through a very tumultuous system of checks and balances, initiatives, contradictions and accommodation. We are governed not by decree but by consent. Such a fragmentary order leaves choice, leaves room for forms of life and building that are not preordained. In short, one should be wary of a unified conception of town form, or at least ready to contradict or invest the prevailing suppositions with fresh imaginings.

Signs of inhabitation are the opposite hand of order. They are the evidence not of controlling and typifying pattern, but of individual adjustment and accommodation, sometimes of protest. If we look for signs of inhabitation, we look for signs that persons are alive and well within the places that have been built—for evidence of special care by the craftsman who inserted a door on the corner, for signs that someone on the third floor still loves plants, for peculiar investments of imagination in carvings, windmills or a most spectacular turret. These signs of inhabitation, together with fragmentary but robust evidence of the wish to order, combine with the simple elements of building that remind us of persons (that is, windows, doors and porches) to present us with a picture of ourselves and our predecessors and of what we might pass on to those who succeed us.

Opportunities for Appropriation

But a place without opportunity is a place to leave. There must be opportunities for each generation to make a structure its own. We've learned, I hope, that these need not be by obliteration. We are learning, it seems, that to understand the effort and care which others have invested and to use it wisely is a form of appropriation. We may best make things our own in ways that do not do violence to what we've inherited. But there must also be slack, room for reinterpretation, place and space for adjustments and new investment. Generally less dense than cities, the small town usually affords such opportunities; indeed at the level of personal decisions in backyards and left-over spaces they often are its greatest strength. Finding opportunity for change at the town scale can be a test of community consciousness.

Providing these three characteristics—distinctness, evidence of the social context, and opportunities for appropriation—can be a guide to policy decisions and physical planning for a town as it faces new pressures. Examining the town from these vantage points and assembling information on its basic forms and patterns can itself be an important step in developing community awareness. To read the town this way is itself a first step towards appropriation or re-appropriation of the town's form and sense and a step away from stereotypes imposed by mass media. Learning to care about what is at hand is the first step in nurture.

To be effective these concerns must govern four levels of organization that make up the town's structure: the division of rights over the land, the types of buildings and their siting, public investments and facilities, and imaginative investment in building form and craft.

The land patterns in a town generally reflect its evolution, and often strange anomalies will appear in lots or even in buildings as a result of conflicting patterns of development in the early plotting or subsequent sale of the land. Efforts to reshape land parcels and access to them are an essential tool for reinterpreting the town structure and making room for new activities. They should, however, be viewed with skepticism and the town should keep careful watch over the allocations of lands and the development rights attached to them. The instruments of zoning have generally been too gross to adequately control the orderly progression of land use change. Automobile-related pressures for the commercial use of land outside the center are particularly problematic in this regard, offering on the one hand new opportunities for business that might otherwise be controlled by established merchants, and on the other visiting real destruction on the existing patterns.

Building types are also subject to change, especially as developments become larger: bigger stores, more houses in a single development. Siting for these buildings and the space between them is often more disruptive than the buildings themselves, especially when there are large areas of associated parking. Each building type in the town should be studied as an element in the streetscape, with particular attention to the ways in which the building adjoins the public space of the town, inviting or rebuffing passersby. New buildings should be evaluated for their fit within the existing chain of events. Often older buildings in the town have latent possibilities for re-use in unaccustomed ways, opportunities which may not be clear when considering one building at a time, but which can be seen if the building type is considered as a group. The upper parts of Main Street commercial

buildings have often benefited from such study, as have light industrial buildings.

Public investments and facilities are an obvious focus for community discussion and concern. They may range from important new
civic buildings or additions to much simpler means of creating fresh
patterns of order. Connecting paths through the block in a way that
reinterprets the street system and provides new access to parking
areas or planting street trees to recover shelter from the sun are
elemental examples. There are several sources for public facilities
work at the local, county, state and federal levels, and small scale
immediate investment should accompany any longer term application
for more remote sources of funds.

In the end the livability of any place depends on the level of
imaginative investment its owners, designers and craftspeople have
been willing or able to make. There are many sources through which
people provoke their imagination. Social ideals have determined the
form of many public buildings, and functional requirements directly
stated have brought forth proud and exciting industrial buildings. The
fully realized demands of the climate have shaped many domestic
buildings, as have the materials of building readily available. Remembered or imagined treasures have perhaps most often motivated
the form and shape of specific buildings. All are legitimate sources,
each best when the others are also present; they really count only
when the source has been overshadowed by the vivacity of the imagined and built response. Buildings can reflect imagination and care
only when those who are responsible are willing to invest it. Then the
street becomes a treasure trove, a worthy setting for our daily specula-
tions regarding what it means to live among neighbors.

Small Town Public Policy:
Strategies for Downtown Revitalization

ROBERT CRAYCROFT

Small towns evoke strong and pleasant images of shady, tree lined streets, neatly kept homes, modest but inviting churches, and, at the center of it all, the downtown. The downtown is the focus of the energy and activity of the small town. It is the place where people go to buy the things they need, to renew acquaintances, to conduct important transactions, to seek diversion and to come together as a community. The downtown carries with it a true "sense of place," born of the town's history. It is the oldest part of town, the intersection of the main streets, and the site of important events. Its architecture has a special quality, built up over a long period of time, in the local manner, by the ancestors of those living. It is the business, social, governmental, and symbolic center of the small town.

Too often, however, such an image is only a nostalgic memory. The common reality is a decaying downtown, its buildings in disrepair, its economy atrophied, its important functions relocated. The neon strip, a gaudy collection of metal buildings and signs, has taken its place. Even the enclosed mall (which in many ways has replaced the town square) is wanting. It is an environment with no particular sense of time or place, not unlike the fast food palaces that line the strip; it is convenient and filling but unsatisfying. A small town cannot support two centers. The strip will thrive only at the expense of the downtown. But if the downtown is allowed to die, the small town is without any *real* center. The strip can only replace the retail function of the downtown; it can replace neither its history nor its symbolism. Deprived of its traditional center, the small town will lose its "sense of place" and be cut adrift.

How does this happen? Can it be prevented? Can the trend be

15

reversed? It is convenient to assume that what has happened to the town was inevitable, that the flow of progress is not to be denied. Values have changed, we are told, and the changes reflect the new values. Inaction in confronting small town pathologies is justified with explanations that the remedies are not within the capabilities of local resources, that massive federal programs are the only solution. It is comforting to think that no one is to blame for what has happened to the small town—it just happened.

But this is not the case. What has happened to the small town is the result of many decisions, made over a long period of time, by the important people who control its destiny. These people are the elected officials, businessmen, civic leaders and influential citizens. None of them planned to do harm to the town they serve. In fact, many of the decisions proving so disastrous to the fate of the small town were actually intended to save it. More often, decisions were made benignly, without consideration of their effects. Only in retrospect do their detrimental consequences come into focus. Ironically, it is these same decisions that constitute the single most effective tool available to the small town in the cause of its revitalization.

There are many variations, but the sequence of events leading to the decline of Main Street is fairly typical. Shortly after World War II, increased automobile use began to clog the streets of small town business districts. The old streets simply were not adequate to accommodate additional traffic. Parking was inadequate and the ambience of the downtown was being destroyed. Merchants demanded, the federal government subsidized, and the local authorities constructed a by-pass highway. The by-pass was intended to save the downtown by relieving it of through traffic. Everyone agreed that it was a good idea.

Gradually a few gas stations were built on the by-pass, followed by a fast-food franchise or two. These developments posed no real threat to the downtown. But they were followed by a few retailers who located there because they wanted a "modern" image, could provide a large amount of free parking, or found it easier and cheaper to build new on the strip rather than remodel their downtown store. This growth culminated with the construction of a chain discount store. No attempt was made to check or control these developments. Main Street merchants didn't really want the competition; civic leaders perceived growth and progress; and shoppers were glad to have an expanded selection of merchandise.

When the shopping center was built, some merchants saw the inevitable and leased space in it; others remained downtown, resigned to getting by the best they could. As buildings fell into disrepair, the professional offices above the stores relocated to new metal buildings with plenty of parking. Curiously, no one seemed to notice the correlation between the rise of the strip and the decline of the downtown.

Meanwhile, the old city hall was beginning to show signs of wear. Since renovation was not popular in those days, a new city hall was built on a large parcel of land several blocks from downtown. Politicians were happy because it was a visible display of tax monies (and it was a good occasion to curry favor with the local building industry). Lawyers moved out to be close to the new civic center. The old city hall was torn down. Other new facilities (the library, police station and community center) were constructed as fine old buildings downtown stood vacant. Deprived of its core patrons, the restaurant closed. Incidental sales to people whose primary destination was city hall were lost.

The stores that did remain downtown failed to keep up with modern shopping trends. Gradually, their clientele (except the poor, elderly, and a few faithful friends) deserted them for the strip. In an attempt to compete with the strip some of the owners decided to "upgrade" the appearance of their shops by installing aluminum fronts over the old brick facades. Others simply ceased maintenance. Empty stores deteriorated until they collapsed. Diseased trees were removed and not replaced. Other trees were cut down to widen the streets and provide more parking. In time, not only was the economic and social importance of the town lost, so also was its character. Main street took on the appearance of a comb with broken teeth, its uniqueness hidden behind an array of false fronts. It became indistinguishable from every other small town suffering the same plight.

This end need not have come to the small towns that share such a history. It could have been prevented had civic leaders been more conscious of the effects of their policies. Indeed, the trend can be reversed if the values and goals of the town are reassessed and creative and aggressive policies put into force.

Small towns do not have the tools for revitalization available to cities, but their problems are not so massive. There is more than a difference of scale between the two, however—there is a qualitative difference. A small town is not just a smaller version of a city—it is a community. In a community, people know each other and can work together to solve their common problems. It is inappropriate to apply urban design methodologies and solutions to small towns. And those in small towns should not feel that they are incapable of undertaking revitalization because they do not have professional planning and design staffs, the ability to grant investment tax incentives, and other tools that cities possess. Most of the problems in a small town are within the comprehension of those living there and can be alleviated within a framework of common sense and forethought.

Many small towns have undertaken clean-up, paint-up revitalization programs. Such efforts are to be applauded, but if no other measures are taken the results will be negligible. Physical revitalization alone cannot change the economic, social, and symbolic well being of Main Street when other, more powerful forces remain unchecked.

The key ingredient to successful downtown revitalization lies in the domain of public policy. Taken singly, no decision has critical impact on the health of the downtown. In the aggregate, such policy decisions *will* reshape the town. It remains for those making policy to direct it to a positive end. They must first formulate an image of what the downtown is to become, then establish goals toward that end. These goals become the standard against which all policy is evaluated. Specific policies should be instituted to further the goals set down and *no* policy should be enacted which is detrimental to their realization. Proposed policies must be carefully examined for long-term effects. They must also be coordinated among the various local bodies and with county, state, and federal agencies to insure that none are working at cross purposes.

The policy and program suggestions set forth here fall into three broad categories: the concentration of energies toward the central business district, the upgrading of the physical fabric of downtown, and making maximum use of local resources. All of these have been implemented in some form in small towns. Seldom have all of them been focused on the effort to save Main Street.

Concentration of Resources

Each time a small town locates a municipal facility away from the downtown area, it contributes to suburbanization. Each time, the functional and social importance of the downtown is reduced. The resources of a small town are too few to be squandered in this way.

Small town government officials must be aware of the relationship that exists between the allocation of civic resources and civic health. Policies should be adopted that concentrate the few available resources. The obvious functions for consideration are those directly related to the municipal government: the city hall, the police department, the library, the community center. County, state, and federal agencies should be persuaded to remain or locate downtown. Equally important are those projects not a part of municipal government but related to it. These include health care facilities and low income and elderly housing projects subsidized by the federal government and sponsored by local agencies.

Strip Zoning

In allowing unlimited development of the retail strip that exists on the perimeter of almost every small town, local governments have virtually decreed the decay of the downtown. The problem is not just the visual chaos wrought by an array of gaudy signs and metal buildings but the creation of direct competition for downtown businesses. Large cities may be able to support multiple shopping centers—small towns cannot.

It is necessary not only to provide incentives to businesses to locate downtown, but to discourage strip development through disincentives or prohibitions. There are, of course, many types of establishments directly related to the automobile which properly belong on the highway, but there are many others which do not. Local planning commissions should distinguish between the two in the creation of a new zoning classification that allows automobile related uses to locate on the strip but places downtown those businesses and services more appropriate to the central business district.

Downtown Development Incentives

Local governments can create conditions conducive to new downtown development. Major retail chains and developers require sizeable parcels for development, adequate parking, and convenient automobile access. New development in the downtown area will not drive local merchants out of business; it will increase their business by returning the entire downtown to its role as *the* center for shopping.

Zoning Regulations

Zoning regulations often prohibit residential occupancies in downtown areas. Such restrictions deny a viable use to existing vacant space. The space above ground floor stores is usually unoccupied, even in towns with a relatively healthy retail trade. Allowing residential uses downtown will provide building owners with an incentive for renovation, increase the value of the structure (consequently raising the tax base), and create a stable downtown population. A permanent downtown population produces revenue for the building owner, becomes a steady clientele for merchants, and acts as a deterrent to crime.

Physical Revitalization

While physical improvements in the central business district cannot in themselves regenerate a decaying downtown, they are necessary in conjunction with the implementation of other programs. Unfortunately, revitalization has gained a poor reputation in many areas because a planner or architect has recommended plans that are not only far beyond the financial capability of most small towns, but are also out of character for the town. Being unable to implement the recommended course of action, the town becomes discouraged and takes no action whatever.

Very few small towns have problems that suggest such drastic solutions. A more appropriate strategy for many small towns is a phased upgrading of the structures combined with a master plan for capital improvements in the public sector to be executed over a period of time. Emphasis should be placed on voluntary commitments by merchants. There should be positive reinforcement for those who make improvements and peer pressure applied to the recalcitrant. Guidelines should be established with the assistance of a preservation planner or architect to ensure a cohesive design.

Improvements to the "Public Floor"

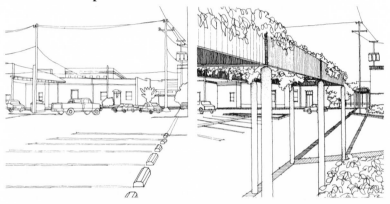

The upgrading of the private wall should be complemented by improvements to the public floor. Sidewalks can be repaired, intersections redesigned to make crossing easier, trees planted, and street furniture installed. Off-street parking behind stores should be upgraded and the link to Main Street made more attractive.

Commitment to Preservation

Public and quasi-public agencies often construct new facilities beyond the boundaries of downtown areas even as structures in or near the central business district go begging. Small towns should follow the enlightened policy of the General Services Administration. Under this policy, the GSA is required to consider the use of space in historic buildings rather than automatically initiate new construction. In the small town this policy should extend beyond historic buildings to any worthwhile structure in the downtown area. Municipal governments should also work to influence county and state agencies to locate downtown, and if necessary remind the federal government of its commitment.

Adaptive use must be aggressively pursued as a means of preserving downtown structures and social vitality. A small town can have only so many museums and historical societies, but through adaptive use it can maintain its character while accommodating growth and progress.

Restoring the Town's Original Character

Historic District Status

Every small town with appropriate building resources should make the effort to be granted status as a Historic District. The benefits of being listed on the National Register of Historic Places are far more than symbolic. The Tax Reform Act of 1976 made the rewards tangible. This law encourages the preservation of old buildings by eliminating the cost of demolition of a structure in a historic district as a tax deduction. On the positive side, the law permits the cost of renovation of commercial properties to be depreciated in only five years (as compared with thirty years for new construction). It also makes private owners eligible for fifty-percent matching grants for renovation work. Even when civic pride or the promise of increased business fail to convince an owner to renovate, tangible financial incentives will make improvement much more likely.

Civic Space

Every small town needs a major civic space downtown. It becomes the focus of community activities from holiday events to farmers markets. The more fortunate towns have a courthouse square, but most towns have no open space within the central business district. When none exists it should be created.

Street Trees Enclose the Space

A vacant lot or the site of a dilapidated structure suggests prime opportunities for such a space. For a relatively minor investment a pleasant park or plaza can be created. The civic space can provide a place of considerable activity and the impetus for eliminating an eyesore. It should be located as near the heart of downtown as possible. If it can be placed adjoining an important civic building, even better.

Unifying Strip Development

Strip development usually occurs along the entry into the downtown proper, and its visual blight does little to enhance the image of Main Street. The chaos associated with most strip developments arises not from the variety (there are many instances in which great variety generates great delight) but from the lack of *any* unifying elements.

Unifying the Strip

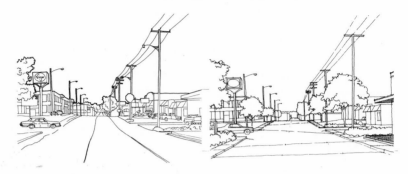

Much of the visual blight can be ameliorated through stringent maintenance of the public domain as a unifying element. Rights-of-way should be treated in a cohesive manner in the development of curbs, sidewalks, ground cover, and street trees. Limitations should be placed on the number, location and size of curb cuts.

Zoning regulations can require that a percentage of the front setback be maintained as landscaped area. Sign ordinances will reduce the visual chaos by limiting the size, type and location of signs. Tree ordinances will protect existing trees by requiring a public hearing before any tree can be cut.

Modernizing Merchandising

Downtown businessmen have done little to slow the demise of the central business district. Often they have refused to acknowledge that they are in competition with the strip. Those who have not abandoned downtown have developed a cynical acquiescence toward their fate, become indifferent toward their customers, and steadfastly refused to adopt modern merchandise and merchandising techniques. Customers gradually abandon downtown businesses because they can find better merchandise, service, and atmosphere elsewhere. This

situation need not occur. If anyone is able to gauge consumer tastes
and provide good service, it should be the local merchant. And no
shopping mall, with all its contrivances, can duplicate the ambience of
Main Street.

Off-Street Parking Upgraded

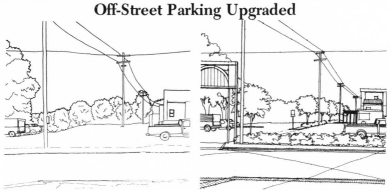

Shopping centers can provide some valuable lessons for local merchants. They need to stop thinking of themselves as a group of individual businesses and start seeing themselves as what they are—part
of a "shopping center." This means more than forming a local merchants organization which is often nothing more than a social club.
They should begin financing improvements to the downtown with
revenues based on a percentage of gross receipts. They should hire a
manager to coordinate joint advertising promotions, recruit new businesses to improve store mix, and organize weekly activities to sup-
plement the shopping experience. They need to familiarize themselves with modern merchandise and merchandising techniques, and
they need to adopt extended hours suitable to the patterns of their
customers. They should make certain that they and their employees
are not taking up the prime parking spaces. Above all, they need to
recognize that shopping and eating should be a pleasure as well as a
necessity and work to create an atmosphere conducive to the shopping experience.

Celebrate Uniqueness

In the headlong rush toward progress many small towns have lost
sight of their identity, that aspect of the town which makes it unique.

In losing its identity, a town loses one of the major ingredients in the enigmatic mix that is "place." It is one of those intangible qualities that make a town a good place to live "in" or be "from."

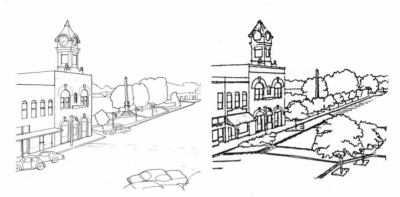

Creating a "Place"

The identity of a town can come from such sources as the town's being the site of a historic event or the home of a famous person. Identity may be related to the original reason for the town's existence; it may focus on a local craft or skill, or it may be derived from the activities of the town's hinterlands. Civic leaders need to rediscover the source of their town's uniqueness and celebrate it. The celebration may be as modest as a mention on the "Welcome to . . ." sign or as ambitious as an all-out annual event. It can become the focus for special merchandising campaigns, school projects, and civic group activities. Celebrating its uniqueness can be a great source of civic pride for the small town and can generate tourism.

Populate the "Place"

A plaza does not make a place. Without social meaning, an open space on Main Street simply becomes a void. Whether a town has a historic "place" or is trying to create one, it must have activity to have any real meaning. The Scouts demonstrate their skills in the parking lots of discount stores, farmers sell produce by the side of the road, and garage sales are held all over town. These activities are capital too precious to be squandered.

A small town does not have a great many activities but it has enough to "people its place." Businessmen and government officials should make every effort to see that what happens, happens downtown. They should organize flea markets and farmers' markets, sponsor arts and crafts fairs, encourage car and tractor dealers to show their new lines, and schedule events by local organizations.

Populating the "Place"

Utilize Community Volunteers

In a city, where people don't know one another, it is difficult to enlist the efforts of private groups in the cause of public sector problems. Individuals or groups can do little that proves meaningful. As a consequence, all the problems occurring in the public sector must be solved by the government. This should not be the case in the small town, for the town can use its one most valuable asset, its sense of community, to solve a great many problems. If civic organizations, church groups, and social clubs coordinate and direct their activities, they can have a visible and meaningful impact on the quality of their environment.

This summary of public policies and programs is not meant to be comprehensive. Neither does it suggest that every small town adopt every policy mentioned. Specific sets of policies must grow from the conditions, resources, and aspirations of the particular situation. Clearly, public policy can have an impact on downtown revitalization; the small town does have the capability to guide its own future. Resignation to decay or reliance on federal programs are not the only alternatives available.

As obvious and beneficial as many of the policy suggestions set forth here may appear, they cannot be put into force without considerable effort on the part of those making policy. Most small towns suffer from negative inertia as the result of years of decline. Small town provincialism and laissez-faire attitudes, which in earlier years were small town strengths, compound the problem. Many proposals will be opposed by special interests which benefit from the status quo. Some programs will require taxation which politicians will be reluctant to propose. Some of these ideas challenge the modern American bias that "new is better than old" and "large is better than small." (Some may even be less than the most efficient, convenient, or economical way of achieving a given objective.)

These obstacles, formidable though they are, must be overcome if small towns are to remain a viable environment in modern America. The long pattern of decline and the attitude of its inevitability must be reversed. Innovative ideas must be generated and evaluated with an open mind. Politicians and civic leaders must face the reality of the situation and make the difficult decisions. Short-term gains must be weighed against long-term effects. Finally, the quality of life must balance quantitative criteria.

Most policy decisions made in the past have been based solely on the basis of efficiency, convenience, and economics. These cannot be the only criteria; they are not measures of the quality of life. Ideas about the quality of life may be subjective and difficult to measure, but they are real and important. They must be a factor in the decision making process. If those making public policy in a small town are serious about restoring it as a good place to live they must establish new priorities and redirect public policy.

NOTE

Illustrations, the result of a team study of West Point, Mississippi, are furnished by Jeffrey Karer, Janet Smith, Anne Robertson, Jan Nelson, Bruce Herrington, Steve Hughes, Janice Woodard, Vicki Ladiner, Sheila Jackson, Reginald Walden and Keith Kirklon.

The Impact of Recent Migrants on Economic Development in Small Towns

EDWARD J. BLAKELY
and
TED K. BRADSHAW

Small towns and rural areas have been characterized for most of this century as depressed, isolated and socially backward.[1] Within this decade, however, rural areas and small nonmetropolitan towns particularly have undergone a remarkable transformation after over half a century of economic and population decline. Since about 1970 small towns have experienced either population stabilization or growth, and their economies have rebounded with an economic resurgence in almost all parts of the United States, Europe and Japan. This new rurality, as some policy makers and scholars are calling it, actually forms what Bradshaw and Blakely have called an emerging advanced rurality in a recent study of rural communities.[2]

The subject of improving conditions of rural areas, first documented by Calvin Beale,[3] is now the focus of much scholarly inquiry. The central thrust of the current research is to "identify the dynamics of the new migration movement."[4] The underlying causes of recent rural inmigration to rural areas is, however, extremely complex. Current research attributes the rural renaissance to several factors. Among them are (1) the quality of rural community life over modern city living;[5] (2) the development of knowledge intensive, high technology industries, such as computer manufacturers and optics that are not raw material or large assembly based;[6] (3) the rising affluence and mobility of the American professional labor force, opting for location over income;[7] (4) increased numbers of affluent, relatively active retirees who prefer both the lower cost and higher quality of living in rural areas;[8] and (5) the dramatic improvement in rural education, social welfare and public services.[9] These factors combined with improved highway and air transportation make rural settings extremely attractive for settlement. The South is not an exception to these trends as it has been to so many other socioeconomic changes in the nation. Quite to the contrary, the prevailing evidence is that the South is a net beneficiary of increased inmigration to both metropolitan and non-metropolitan areas. Southern nonmetropolitan communities received more than a million new manufacturing jobs between 1962 and 1978, or more than half of all the new jobs created in smaller labor market areas during the period.[10] This revitalization of Southern nonmetropolitan communities can be attributed in part to the movement of low wage industrial activity from the North and Northeast to the South, but also to a significant improvement in service sector and high technology industries in the region as well. Nonetheless, the precise mix of forces and factors contributing to recent growth of small towns and rural areas is not well understood.

The purpose of this paper is to (1) provide a conceptual framework for understanding the current trends in rural growth; (2) examine the role newcomers play in the changing economic base of rural areas; and (3) suggest some alternatives available to small town public officials and community leaders to plan effectively for these changes.

The Small Town in an Advanced Industrial Society

The focus of research on rural areas heretofore has been on the gaps, lags, needs and desperation of rural areas. The fate of small town America has been connected to the demise of the family farm and exhaustion and non-renewable forest and energy resources. Today, by contrast, there is increasing evidence that rural America is undergoing a broad and fundamental change in its basic socioeconomic structure.[11] Rural areas once thought of as pastoral and agricultural or based on extractive industry are rapidly moving away from this depiction toward more balanced and robust economies. Only a small percentage of rural populations continue to make their living from farming. New high technology and knowledge intensive industry, tourism, and service organizations are forming a large part of what is coming to be termed postindustrial or advanced industrial rural society.[12] As a result, the disparity in quality of life indicators that formerly existed between rural regions and urban areas is diminishing. Recent research by Bradshaw and Blakely in *Rural Communities in Advanced Industrial Society* on nonmetropolitan California indicates that rural areas may well be in an advantageous position to become the "new frontier" for the advanced industrialism. As a result, rural areas are becoming the focal point of a movement away from a raw-material-based industrialism toward a new human-resource-based economic structure.

This new rural economic model is characterized, as shown on the following chart, by increased emphasis on skilled human resources for the generation of new wealth rather than the exploitation of non-renewable resources. The former disparities in educational, social service and social amenities in rural areas is moderating as a result of the federal grant and aid structure. In fact, some recent social indicators data compiled by Peggy J. Ross and others[13] of the U. S. Department of Agriculture indicate the gap in social well-being between metropolitan and nonmetropolitan residents is rapidly diminishing. In addition, in their 1979 study Bradshaw and Blakely provide evidence that rural government structures have been augmented and amplified through better linkage with regional as well as national governmental structures. As a result, an interdependent politico-economic network is being forged which provides small towns with improved capacity to manage their destinies. Finally, professional planners, community developers and other social technologists are expanding options and opportunities for improved quality of life in rural areas.

Thus small towns are conducive to a new form of economic growth. In order to understand the changing character of small towns, we must reorient our thinking, our research paradigms and our policy foci away from concepts of rural poverty, economic lag and depression toward a conceptualization of nonmetropolitan America as an area with potential new frontiers for the expansion of the advanced industrial society.

Themes of Reverse Migration Research

The notion of an advanced rural society provides a framework for understanding the phenomenon of recent rural growth. This concept is supported by the three following current research thrusts.

Characteristics of the Industrial Society, the Advanced Industrial Society, and Rural areas of the Advanced Industrial Society

Characteristic	Industrial Society	Advanced Industrial	Rural Advanced Industrial
Technology	High energy consuming machinery substituted for human labor	Knowledge intensive technologies substituted for bulky machinery	Knowledge intensive agriculture in a highly integrated food industry; movement of electronics and other high technology plants to the rural area.
Services	Services introduced to the marketplace; growth of transportation, utilities, communication and trade	Professionalized and extensive network providing specialized services.	Specialized agricultural service; expanded tourism; and wider distribution of professional and welfare services.
Knowledge	Development of literacy and mass primary schooling	Nearly universal higher education and extensive institutionalized research network.	Better distribution of educational opportunities; research taking place on farms; new educational structures outside of schools; new atmosphere of need and interest in education.
Relationships	Traditional relations replaced by rationalism and secular concerns	High degree of interdependence and complexity which demands planning and coordination	Rural towns integrated into regional networks; media create increasing awareness of outside developments; emergence of regional governmental systems.

Source: Bradshaw and Blakely, *Rural Communities in Advanced Industrial Society.*

Preferences of Community Size. This research has focused on the preferences of settlement for most Americans. Work in this area by Don A. Dilman and Russell Dobosh, as well as that by Glenn V. Fuguitt and James Zuiches,[14] provides insights into the quality of life factors in nonmetropolitan areas that make them the choice of many Americans for permanent residence. The data indicate that the majority of Americans prefer small town environments within reasonable range of metropolitan centers.

Formerly, the limited economic opportunities in small towns acted as impediments to exercising this option. The recent movement of business and industrial firms to rural areas, however, has substantially reduced this barrier to community choice.[15] In addition to individual preferences, business and industry find small town locations beneficial as well. Wolfgang Quante and other researchers have found that small towns offer more flexible government systems, cheaper land and a superior labor supply.[16] The combination of individual desires and business interest makes nonmetropolitan areas extremely attractive.

The New Migrants. The actual flow of new inmigrants to rural areas, Louis Ploch observed, may not be as important as the characteristics of the migrants themselves. Recent evidence indicates that new migrants to rural areas, compared to established residents, tend to be better educated and enter professional and managerial occupations. This demographic phenomenon appears to be occurring in all areas experiencing growth. For example, Ploch indicates that 38 percent of the male heads of household among inmigrants in Maine were in professional, managerial and similar fields.[17] Similarly, Bradshaw and Blakely in *Rural Communities in Advanced Industrial Society* show that professionals such as engineers and scientists represent a substantial portion of rural population growth in California. This pattern is true for the bulk of the recent growth in the South. Gladys Bowles points out that "just over two-fifths of the employed white male metro/nonmetro migrants were in white collar occupations and two-fifths were in blue collar jobs."[18]

The increased access of rural areas to higher education resources, Bradshaw suggests, is a significant factor in the movement of professionals to nonmetropolitan areas.[19] The community college, as well as the upgrading of former state teachers' colleges to university status, provides a base that supports high intelligence industrial growth such as telecommunications and computers. In addition, these institutions provide avenues for the migrants' continuing intellectual growth and broader educational opportunities for their children.[20] Finally, community colleges and universities also provide a substantial cadre of trained personnel to serve as consultants and part time employees to support business and industrial expansion.

The Socio-political Impacts of Growth. There is increasing evidence that there are some attitudinal differences between the new inmigrants and the existing population. For example, Lawrence Hennigh shows that a crisis over the funding of local schools in several small towns in Oregon was precipitated by a fundamental clash in beliefs regarding the functions of the school system.[21] Similarly, others have shown how newcomers and old timers have divergent attitudes toward population and choice of industry for economic growth, the newcomers generally favoring more restrained or planned population growth and a narrower range of industrial or agricultural opportunities than long time residents.[22] Finally, Alvin Sokolow and others have indicated that newcomers fit well into the small town political life.[23] However, their expectations of local government differ from those of the old timers in several respects. The newcomers' earlier experiences of urban government, its capacity and services, provide the framework for the inmigrants' conception of government. Regardless of perceived or real concerns about government services, the newcomers share with the existing residents a desire to keep local government small.[24]

In sum, the increased demands of new migrants for improved government services combined with their political experience with complicated bureaucracy has led to dramatic improvements in the quality of small town governments. This in turn allows the new migrants to make few adjustments in their life styles or their expectations of government.

The three themes discussed above suggest that the affluence of modern America provides a new opportunity for people to act out their settlement preferences. At the same time, the shift in the economic system to a knowledge intensive, high technology and service oriented character, places a premium on human resources. Thus, as individuals exercise their settlement options, business and industry follow rather than precede them. As a related consequence, the increased demands on education, social welfare and local government combined with an improved tax base, bring about accelerated improvements in local government services.

The concepts previously discussed lead to another important component in sketching the notion of an advanced rural society. The economic contribution of the inmigrant is central to understanding the capacity of small communities to maintain growth. It is also linked to the fundamental premise that human resources and not raw materials form the base of the new economic structure. There are several components to this argument. First, the inmigrants form the base of a well educated and capable labor force. Second, they are able to find suitable employment. Third, the inmigrants are presumed to create wealth by starting or improving local enterprises. Finally, the inmigrants' contribution to the local small town economy is greater than their demands for public services. In short, they are not a social welfare dependent population. These components of the economic development theme are considered in the balance of this paper because they address the important questions of how so many new people are able to sustain themselves in rural areas.

A Typology of Growth Communities

It seems clear that several different types of small towns are experiencing growth. As Louis Ploch suggests, "Each sociocultural area has characteristics which will serve as a selected attractive force to potential inmigrants."[25] That is, a certain degree of growth specialization is occurring among small towns and nonmetropolitan areas. This specialization seems to be synergistic inasmuch as the migration pattern to the communities reinforces its cultural, economic and political direction, consequently attracting more people of similar backgrounds. For example, retirement communities in the Sun Belt build retiree social facilities and programs and thereby attract more retirees.

The same phenomena are operating in rural industrial development as well. Thus, knowledge intensive industry tends to locate near highly skilled personnel, which attracts more such persons. We have identified six specialized types of growth communities.

Tourism/Recreation Communities. These areas are usually noted for their scenic beauty. Usually the inmigrants are economically independent with most of the residents possessing highly portable and lucrative skills in managing real estate, writing, publishing or tourism management. Within the South, the Carolinas and Florida recreation communities are the best examples of the recent growth of this type.

Professional Service Communities. These communities generally have a higher education institution as their base. While some of these communities have a four year state university, most have undergone growth recently due to the development of two year community colleges. These communities are the home of knowledge intensive industries such as computers and optics as well as professions such as law, accounting, and engineering. The research triangle in the Raleigh, North Carolina, area is a good illustration of this form of growth, as is Blacksburg, Virginia.

Mixed Economy Trade Communities. Construction, agricultural processing or a similar economic base drives the economy of these small towns. The national highway system has made many of these areas more accessible than they previously were. Further, most of these cities serve as centers of government, financial and similar institutions.

Retirement Communities. The economic activity is principally that of providing services to retirees. These communities are also usually places with year round recreation. In many cases, they are located in mild climates. Virginia, Florida, and the Carolinas have chiefly benefited from this movement, as have many areas of Tennessee, Arkansas and Mississippi.

Counter Culture Communities. Economic activity in these communities is linked to life style services rather than the generation of wealth. These communities are primarily in the Southwest and far West. The craft oriented communities not too distant from population centers like New Orleans and Atlanta best exemplify this type of community.

Energy Boom Town. These new communities, created almost overnight to capitalize on exploration of some mineral or other power sources, are nearly all in the intermountain states. The research reported here will depict the economic contribution of new migrants of the first five community types. The Energy Boom Towns are not discussed because they are more an illustration of the old raw-material oriented economic system in a new setting. Further, there are few such communities in California where this research was conducted nor is it characteristic of the pattern in most of the South.

In the next section, we discuss consequences of the economic contribution of inmigrants for rural development. Although this research was conducted in California, one should not attempt to draw too much or too little from it. There is a tendency to embrace occurrences in California as the wave of the future or dismiss them as the peculiarities of a bizarre population. In this research, we believe California is a good illustration or barometer of the future and not an unusual or atypical example. Rural California is clearly influenced by the urbanism of the state, but it has developed its own unique character and strong independent economic base. Thus it is both illustrative of the nationwide trend and is a trend setter.

Research Setting and Approach

The research procedure was to administer questionnaires in person to newcomers in California communities characteristic of the five types discussed previously. The requisite diversity of communities was found in two northern counties experiencing particularly rapid population growth: Butte and Mendocino counties. These two areas are located in the northern quarter of California and are counties that have been dependent on lumber, ranching and farming as their economic base. These bases are rapidly declining. Each county has specialized agricultural fruit crops, Butte County in tree fruits and Mendocino in wine grapes. The population growth in these areas has followed the pattern described and is largely due to the attractiveness of the areas, combined with their relatively easy access to the San Francisco and Sacramento urban areas (two to four hours away by car).

The communities chosen for the survey include the town of Mendocino (Mendocino County). It is a spectacular, historic coastal community with several nearby state parks, a significant artist colony, and a growing tourist industry. Chico (Butte County) was selected as an example of a rapidly growing valley community with a campus of the California State University system. It also acts as the professional services center in medicine, law, engineering, government and the arts for northeastern California. Oroville, the county seat of Butte County, represents a growing trade, nonprofessional and government service center. It is a service community for many recreational and retirement settlements in the nearby mountains, and has a traditional industrial and construction base, as a result of the recent construction of the Oroville Dam. Paradise, a third Butte County community, was included in the study because it is a rapidly growing retirement location where developers appealed to potential migrants from Los Angeles with television ads that pictured this delightful forested setting and mild climate. Finally, the Mendocino mountain communities of Boonville, Philo, and Comptche are centers of countercultural life styles where the early dropouts from San Francisco's "hippy" community moved back to the land to cultivate vegetables, cannabis and other crops and to lead simple lives.

The research procedure was simple and straightforward. Questionnaires were administered to a sample of newcomers in each of these five areas by trained interviewers. About fifty interviews were conducted in each area, providing a total of 241 usable responses. Using maps of each area, streets were listed and selected randomly. (Long streets were divided into several segments.) On each street interviewers were provided a random starting place and called on houses until they located a newcomer. Newcomers were arbitrarily defined as residents of a particular rural county for between one and five years. If the household did not qualify, residents were asked whether they knew of any newcomers on the street. These references were pursued. Quotas of between two and four completed interviews were set for each street, depending on the number of houses on the street or segment of street. Each interview took about thirty minutes. Interviewees were queried about their reasons for moving, their personal backgrounds, employment experiences in the community and use of community services. An overall cooperation rate of over 90 percent was achieved. The data presented here are preliminary results and may be subject to slight modification. Data are not segmented by community in this presentation.

Results

The recent migrants to California's small towns are typical of other migrants to rural areas who have been studied by other researchers. They were better educated than the long time residents. A significantly high precentage of newcomers were in professional occupations. In general, these data confirm the basic treatise. (1) The primary motivation for migrating to rural areas was to pursue a rural lifestyle even though economic conditions were generally less desirable for the migrant. (2) The new migrants, however, were able to use their employment skills and to make a significant contribution to the economic growth of these areas. (3) The migrants were able to use their abilities to a large extent by starting their own businesses, largely small, individual activities. The newcomers' abilities rather than any raw material formed the base for business expansion. (4) Finally, the newcomers were largely a non-dependent group, using few unemployment or other services.

A Migration of People with Resources. The data clearly show that the bulk of the recent migrants came from urban areas. The majority (74 percent) came from urban or suburban locations while the remaining (25 percent) came from other small towns or farms. Most of the migrants moved from other California counties, although 20 percent came from out-of-state locations scattered in 25 states. The migration from urban areas provides the most significant resource for rural economic growth.

The primary motive for newcomers to move to the small town areas of California is the chance to pursue a rural life style, rather than economic or employment opportunities. Some had retired already and had no interest in working. Our sample included 23 percent retired persons. Working persons, however, also strongly favored lifestyle values over work.

Data presented in Table 1 illustrate this point. Respondents were asked the extent to which various factors were favorable in their decision to move to their new community. At the same time that less than half of the working respondents found economic factors favorable only 16 percent indicated that they considered their job prospects as an unfavorable factor in their decision to move.

Table 1

**Percent Reporting Factor Favorable to
Decision to Move to Rural County**

	Working	Retired	Total
Climate or geography	72	88	76
Rural Atmosphere	85	89	86
Simplicity of life	75	78	75
Job prospects	41	3	28
New business or job potential	49	3	34
(N)	(199)	(64)	(241)*

*Includes 28 unemployed or otherwise not in labor force.

The new migrants are a well educated and highly skilled group. Among heads of household over 65 percent have had some college training. Table 2 presents the data on the level of education of the respondents. Interestingly, the newcomers who were working included 6.7 percent with masters' degrees and 8.1 percent with Ph.Ds'.

Table 2

Educational Level of Newcomers

	Working	Retired	Total
Less than high school	4.7%	28.1%	12.9%
High school graduate	16.8	29.7	21.2
College, some BA	63.0	34.4	54.0
MA, PhD	14.8	6.3	11.2

The newcomers provided a substantial transfer of economic resources when they moved. Six out of ten newcomers reported savings of well over $1,000, and nearly 40 percent had in excess of $1,000 from the sale of a house. These and other major income resources were available to 71 percent of the respondents.

Successful Employment. The migration of highly skilled workers to rural areas is considered improbable according to current economic theory. Employment opportunities are supposedly not available and the conditions necessary for the use of highly skilled persons are assumed to be remote. The question to be addressed here is why these skilled workers migrated and how they succeeded in developing employment in the small town economic system.

There were three primary patterns of locating a job among migrants. First, about 7 percent of the workers were transferred by their employer from another county. Another 34 percent arranged their job before moving, such as college professors in Chico. The remainder, 55 percent, sought their job after coming to the county. The job search, however, often included moving from one job to another. Over 48 percent of the employed migrants reported having taken another job since moving to the rural area.

The lack of industrial employment for new migrants is clearly evident in employment data in Table 3. Only 10.6 percent of the newcomers are employed in manufacturing. Another 7.7 percent are employed in agriculture, primarily in specialized agricultural services. The rest are employed in construction or service industries.

It is interesting to note that the largest industrial category is professional employment with 22.6 percent of the newcomers in such industries as those providing health care and schooling. Government, however, provided employment for only 3.6 percent of the newcomers even though rural governmental employment has been substantial throughout the country. Proposition 13, a voter enacted tax limitation initiative which greatly limited local tax revenues, might have contributed to this low figure in government employment.

Table 3

Industry of Employment, Recent Migrants

Agriculture	7.7%
Mining/Construction	13.4
Manufacturing	10.6
Transportation, Utilities	4.7
Trade	14.9
Finance Insurance Real Estate	3.6
Services	5.9
Professional industries	22.6
Government	3.6

In terms of occupation we found that 28.8 percent of the newcomers were employed in professional managerial or technical jobs. Almost one in six (16.8 percent) of the newcomers worked as sales persons or clerks and one in five worked as food preparers or servers, or protective service workers. Another large occupational category included construction workers or truck drivers (22.1 percent). Only 9 percent of the sample worked in production as machine operators or attendants and none were laborers.

The industrial and occupational patterns of the new migrants suggest they would work in small businesses serving local needs. Only one quarter of the places of employment were part of a corporate chain or multi-location business that extended out of the county. Another 20 percent worked in businesses with more than one local location. In part this reflects the recent economic growth in these rural counties. Over 40 percent of the places of employment have not been in existence in the same community for over five years. Thus, employees have found employment in new small businesses.

Table 4
Median Income Newcomers

Male head of household, one income	11,000 - 11,999	N=63
Male head of household, two incomes	13,000 - 24,999	N=53
Female head of household	4,000 - 4,999	N=27
Retired	11,000 - 11,999	N=64

Among all newcomer interviewees, the median family income was between $11,000 and $11,999. The primary source of income was wages for the employed workers and social security for the retired and disabled. Individual income earned by the head of household was supplemented by spouses' earnings in many cases. Spouse employment was identified in 42 percent of the cases where the breadwinner was married; female employment experiences were similar to those of the male head of household. Retirees had higher incomes than anticipated. In spite of higher incomes, retirees did not have supplemental employment, which indicated pensions and investments were sufficient to sustain them.

In summary, the data indicate that the new migrants were highly skilled and successful in finding a place for themselves in the new rural economy. On the whole it may be assumed that this would be the case because those who could not make it during the first year would leave and we would not interview them. However, we also identified a good fit between the job the newcomers had and their perception of their qualifications. About 70 percent reported that their present job was about right for a person of their qualifications and 3.4 percent said they were underqualified. The remaining quarter reported that they were overqualified. This small number may not really reflect the situation since well qualified individuals in some fields currently are accepting employment below their skill level. Further, as skills increase, the size of the enterprises in rural areas may become a real barrier to personal growth.

Table 5
Percent Migrants Starting Business in New Rural County

	Working	Other	Retired	Total
Place of primary employment	36.9	10.7	1.6	24.5
Other business started (e.g. investment)	6.7	3.6	1.6	5.0
Attempt or business failure	4.0	7.1	3.2	4.2
Total business started	47.6	21.4	6.4	33.7
N	(149)	(28)	(64)	(241)

Migrants and Small Business Development. One of the significant results of this research is the discovery that nearly 35 percent of the entire sample started a business in their new rural county. Table 5 shows the results of this question. Further questions determined that these businesses were for the most part single family efforts where the individual was involved in every step including planning, financing, management, and daily operation as well. The businesses were not the primary reason the migrants located in their rural county—more decided to open the business *after* moving than decided to open it before moving. The attraction of the area seemed to be personal reasons such as liking the area or having always wanted to open a business. Low wages or low taxes hardly figured for most people. In short, the data suggest that about a third of the people opening businesses simply stumbled into them and now are making a significant contribution to the rural economy through their efforts.

The impact of these data is to emphasize that rural migrants are a net resource for new kinds of economic development in rural California. Instead of an emphasis on economic growth through attracting industry, the new migrants are a resource for considerable economic stimulation.

Dependency. In general, the findings show that the new migrants are not a dependent group. Community resource structures do contribute valuable assistance to many new migrants. For example, 22.6 percent of the working primary breadwinners report having received unemployment insurance, and 19.5 percent of the spouses collected payments. Yet only 9 percent report that public assistance is a source of over $500 during the last year, and less than 2 percent report that assistance is a primary source of income.

A primary motive for moving to rural areas among our respondents was a desire to be "self-sufficient," to reduce dependence on government and urban institutions. The data indicate that the urbanites who come to the rural areas neither use nor need public support. The greatest need was by retired persons for senior citizen information referral, or nutrition services. Only one in five persons reported having received public assistance, welfare or food stamps since coming to the county. However, over a quarter used public medical assistance.

One of the major uses of public facilities was for training programs to improve job performance. About 29 percent of the sample reported taking noncredit courses in the rural county. This use underscores the role of improved higher education resources in rural economic development. Among the workers 26 percent reported taking training in their rural community to improve their job skills.

Conclusion

It is clear that the newcomers form an important new economic resource for their communities. They bring to the community employment skills as well as professional backgrounds which enable them either to find or create employment. This finding is important because it runs almost directly counter to the prevailing view of personal economic choice. That is, employment opportunity is not the primary motivation for this form of migration; rather, the quality of community life represents the principal consideration in their economic choice.

One must be careful not to draw too hasty a conclusion from these data. As noted earlier, the newcomers had substantial economic resources when they moved. Clearly, this seems to be a selected movement of highly qualified and economically stable groups.

Rural developers have focused their energies for at least four decades on creating industrial opportunities in rural areas. Ideas such as growth centers, improved transportation systems, industrial parks and tax deferrals have been part of the arsenal of those attempting to improve rural economic conditions. These activities have stimulated few real changes in rural conditions.

Now these conditions—smallness, rural life styles and some isolation from urban areas—are suddenly assets. The change is confounding and confusing economists, planners, and developers. How does one maintain the old atmosphere while improving such physical facilities as housing, sewers, shopping areas, recreation facilities, hospitals and public services? Planners have not been particularly adept at this form of planning activity, and citizens have taken matters into their own hands. For example, Petaluma, California, as well as several of the communities we studied, are considering growth limitations, though growth limits are no real answer to preserving community environment. In fact, they have such negative features as driving up housing prices and pushing out service personnel like school teachers, government employees, hotel and restaurant personnel and others. Clearly this effect is undesirable.

Growth management for small communities is a new phenomenon which requires consideration of several important factors.

Human Resource Attraction. Since human resources form such an important element in community growth, communities should decide what type of persons fit into their community. Planners and policy makers should deemphasize industrial attraction schemes and put their efforts into making their communities attractive to selected populations.

Dean MacCannell in *The Tourist* shows how places, like communities can identify themselves and thus become attractive for certain kinds of people.[26] This is a radical notion because it suggests the old industrial development model is no longer viable. The tax breaks for business and other concepts, we argue, should be abandoned in favor of people oriented planning.

Small Town Government Capacity. Small town government must be ready to respond to these rapid changes. The newcomers expect responsive government, though in the past small towns have not had the raison d'etre or opportunity to be creative in their responses to the citizenry. The newcomers' demands for new or improved physical facilities have to be blended into the community setting. It is important that city officials not build an urban type of physical environment in their attempts to keep pace with growth and thus destroy the very environment that stimulated the growth.

Role of Education Resources. Education is perhaps the most critical component in nonmetropolitan growth. The availability of good elementary schools is important, but the most important educational resource is the community college or technical institute. Local policy makers should consider education and, in some instances, health facilities as the centerpiece in their community planning efforts.

Small Town Architecture and Town Planning. Historical preservation has gained tremendous acceptance in small towns, but in most rural small communities the cost of preserving many old structures is prohibitive. Further, the old buildings are usually a jumble of designs from various periods with no theme. It thus makes more sense to consider a theme for the community and build around it. Preservation can be included in the architecture and planning of small towns, but it should be consistent with a central theme.

In the past, business decided architectural design, as exemplified by shopping centers and industrial parks. It is more sensible now to build architecture and town plans around life style dimensions, which should be used in planning such locations as those of bike paths and shopping and recreation areas.[27]

In summary, the emergence of the small town as an economic and population growth area may be a signal that new factors are shaping our economy. Life style, we argue, is becoming a significant factor in shaping a new advanced industrial society. A new rurality is emerging from this process and it may well form a new frontier for America's twenty-first century.

NOTES

[1]See *People Left Behind*, President's National Commission on Rural Poverty (Washington, D.C.: GPO, 1967).

[2]Ted K. Bradshaw and Edward J. Blakely, *Rural Communities in Advanced Industrial Society* (New York: Praeger, 1979).

[3]Calvin L. Beale, "The Revival of Population Growth in Nonmetropolitan America," Economic Research Service Publication No. 605 (Washington, D.C.: U. S. Dept. of Agriculture, 1975).

[4]Louis A. Ploch, "The Reversal in Migration Patterns—Some Rural Development Consequences," *Rural Sociology*, 43 (Summer 1978), 294.

[5]See James J. Zuiches, "Inmigration and Growth of Nonmetropolitan Urban Places," *Rural Sociology*, 35 (Sept. 1970), 410–20.

[6]See M. F. Petrulis, "Growth Patterns in Nonmetro Manufacturing Employment," Rural Development Research Report 7 (Washington, D.C.: U. S. Dept. of Agriculture: Economics, Statistics and Cooperative Service, 1979); Richard E. Lonsdale and H. L. Seyler, *Nonmetropolitan Industrialization* (Washington, D.C.: Winston and Sons, 1979), p. 186; and Robert L. Wrigley, "Small Cities Can Help to Revitalize Rural Areas," *Annals*, Jan. 1973, p. 59.

[7]See Peter A. Morrison and Judith Wheeler, "Rural Renaissance in America," (Washington, D.C.: Population Reference Bureau, 1976); Ted K. Bradshaw and Edward J. Blakely, *Policy Implications of Changing California Life Styles* (Berkeley: Institute of Governmental Studies, 1978); and Gladys K. Bowles, "Contribution of Recent Metro/Nonmetro Migrants to Nonmetro Population and Labor Force," *Agricultural Economic Research*, 30 (Oct. 1978), 15–22.

[8]Edward J. Blakely, "Goal Setting for Community Development: The Case of Yuba City, California" (Davis, Ca.: Institute of Governmental Affairs, 1978).

[9]See Bradshaw and Blakely, *Rural Communities in Advanced Industrial Society.*

[10]Lonsdale and Seyler, p. 43.

[11]Harry K. Schwarzweller, "Migration and the Changing Rural Scene," *Rural Sociology*, 44 (Spring 1979), 7.

[12]Ted K. Bradshaw, "The Rural Advanced Industrial Society: Social and Economic Change," paper presented at American Sociological Society, Boston, Aug. 1979.

[13]See Peggy J. Ross, Herman Bluestone and Fred K. Hines, "Indicators of Social Well Being," Rural Development Research Report No. 10 (Washington, D.C.: U. S. Department of Agriculture: Economics, Statistics and Cooperative Services, 1979).

[14]See Don A. Dilman and Russell Dobosh, "Preferences for Community Living and Their Implications for Population Redistribution" (Pullman, Wa.: College of Agriculture, Washington State Univ., 1972); Glenn V. Fuguitt and James Zuiches, "Residential Preferences and Population Distribution," paper presented at Meetings of Rural Sociological Society, 1973.

[15]See Andrew Sofranko, James D. Williams, Frederick C. Fliegel, "Urban Migrants to the Rural Midwest: Some Understandings" (Ames, Iowa: North Central Center for Rural Development, 1978).

[16]See Wolfgang Quante, *The Exodus of Corporate Headquarters from New York City* (New York: Praeger, 1976).

[17]Ploch, pp. 294–95.

[18]Bowles, p. 17.

[19]Bradshaw, "Rural Advanced Industrial Society."

[20]See James G. Paltridge, Mary Regan and Dawn Terkla, *Mid Career Change: Adult Students in Mid Career Transition and Community Support Developed to Meet Their Needs* (Washington, D.C.: Office of Education, Community Service and Continuing Education Division, 1978).

[21]Lawrence Hennigh, "The Good Life and the Taxpayers' Revolt," *Rural Sociology*, 43 (1978), 178–90.

[22]See Blakely, "Goal Setting for Community Development," and Robert W. Marans and John D. Wellman, *The Quality of Nonmetropolitan Living: Evaluation, Behavior and Expectations of Northern Michigan Residents* (Ann Arbor: Survey Research Center, Institute of Social Research, Univ. of Michigan, 1978).

[23]See Alvin D. Sokolow, "The Politics of Small Town Growth—Newcomers, Issues and Local Government," paper presented at Conference on Understanding Population Change, Urbana-Champaign, Il., March 1979.

[24]See Blakely, "Goal Setting for Community Development."

[25]Ploch, p. 294.

[26]*The Tourist—A New Theory of the Leisure Class* (New York: Schocken, 1976).

[27]Teresa Zogby, "Mixed Use Districts," *PAS Memo* of the American Planning Association, 79 (11) Nov. 1979, 3.

Adversity and Change in Small Town and Rural Area Planning:
State and Local Management Responses in Kansas

JOHN W. KELLER and RAY B. WEISENBURGER

So many events in the field of state and local planning have come about so quickly in the past decade that we, the professional planners, find ourselves prominently involved in one of the great issues of this century. Sweeping reforms, already instituted in virtually every state, are underway to restructure the relationship of man to his natural and built environment. A tremendous range of plans, management techniques, regulatory powers and policies are being effectively coordinated so that generations yet unborn will have an opportunity to benefit from the immense stock of resources we now possess.

From our standpoint, there is unfortunately a void in the plans, policies and reforms of state government. Virtually no allowance has been made for policies governing rural development or for fresh approaches to the problems experienced by the small, non-metropolitan communities. Although the new mood in state government is to involve the rural areas, since these areas contain the very resources the states are trying to protect, the focus is upon the natural environment and the management of populations rather than the physical and social needs of small communities. These communities are forced to take on the added burdens of plan and policy preparation at a time when they scarcely have the ability to repair their aging public facilities. State plans do nothing to take away the burdens of the small localities; at most, they make the communities feel more important as they continue their downhill slide.

Little is being done to solve these problems principally because there are few willing to address them. The rural community planning specialist is one of the rare practitioners in the profession today. The problems seem so vast and insurmountable, the resources so few, and the rewards so scarce, that the few young planners who might have potential interest cannot be attracted away from the metropolitan and state agencies.

Kansas presents a paradigm of these problems, for it is a state of small towns. Within its borders, every known problem of the small community can be found. Understanding these problems is, of course, the requisite to a fresh approach.

Today's problems in a typical rural Kansas community are one hundred years old. To deal effectively with them requires an understanding of the community's function, why it was settled, why it was located where it was, and what its relationship is to surrounding communities.

The answers to these questions are both simple and complex in a world of expanding urbanism and metropolitan growth. Many of the Midwestern and Western states developed as a result of a rectangular planning technique, private incentives backed by public investment, and an uncoordinated settlement policy promulgated by the federal government for nearly eighty years.

Kansas is land—52,000,000 acres of it. It was a territory that federal policy dictated should not be settled and was therefore reserved and held in trust for a large number of American Indian tribal governments. The Homestead Laws quickly changed this policy and much of the state was opened to settlement before a survey was undertaken.[1]

Kansas is one of America's foremost examples of the grid planning technique. Counties are divided into a fairly even number of townships, which, delineated by tiers and ranges, are in turn divided into 36 sections each. The overall planning scheme was to provide for public services, schools, churches, cemeteries, and government facilities in such a way that they were centrally located and accessible to all residents of the townships. Sections 16 and 36 were set aside for education purposes and other public uses, the intention being that no person would be more than four miles from public facilities. The original planners envisioned the eventual growth of the townships and planned an appropriate land use design that would unfold as the population grew.

The inhabitants and investors in the Homestead states did not, however, detect this physical plan. Each person or family was entitled to 160 acres for $1.25 per acre (eventually $2.25) and an additional land area of 40 acre parcels, as long as they were contiguous.[2] Investors and private groups could purchase up to 5,000 acres for land on which to incorporate a municipality; the general land area requested for purchase was 320 acres, the minimum allowed under the Homestead guides.

When the railroads came to Kansas, eagerly supported by the General Assembly, so enthusiastic was the Assembly that it eventually arranged for the different railroad corporations to acquire almost one-fifth of the land area of the state, 10,000,000 acres.[3] In the rush to grant the railroad lands that were held in trust for various Indian tribes, 500,000 acres of land that was granted to Kansas for educational purposes was also included in the package.

The railroad corporations offered reduced fare excursions to farmers interested in settling the agricultural lands or to lot or commercial purchasers in their new towns. Investment companies offered lucrative deals in their instant communities to potential settlers. The federal government offered land rushes, land auctions, and payment in land for military service. Combined with this were communities locating in response to cattle trails, wagon trails, numerous military forts and reservations, and the early missions.

Within the space of a few decades many small towns were established. A very few, because of their desirable locations, continued to grow as trade centers within their geographic areas. Most reached their population peak in the period between 1890–1920 and have continued to decline since.

The lack of forethought that went into the location of many communities, with the eventual infrastructure of water lines, sewers, streets, hospitals, schools (which were in competition with the township schools), and other public facilities, has brought us to our present circumstances. These communities have far too much money invested in them to make any sweeping policy of resettlement feasible, but their remote location and lack of quality facilities make it impossible for them to function effectively.

Before discussing the major problems of small towns, we should note three major restraints on solutions to these problems.

Participation. There is a keen competition for the time of persons willing to participate in community affairs in small communities. Small communities have all of the activities—social, cultural and developmental—that exist in their urban counterparts. Because of the smaller population, however, the number of memberships per person is much higher in the rural community, with the result that community involvement means pulling persons away from other social or civic obligations.

The Error Effect. One prerequisite for a problem solving approach is an adequate data base. Rural communities seldom generate any primary information of their own. Some plans have been prepared for rural areas under the "701" program or as part of an old Economic Development district; unfortunately, much of this information is inaccurate.

Resistance. Many residents and local officials of rural America have a narrow view of community development. A community-based development program, coordinated through the state and region, requires comprehensive planning and structured community changes. Since many changes are regulatory in nature, there is a constant source of internal resistance.

With these restraints in mind, we can identify the major problems concerning (a) declining economic base, (b) change in the composition of the population as well as the size, (c) diminishing transportation and communication facilities, (d) continued indifference to the environment, and (e) voids in leadership. We should like to examine each of these briefly.

Economic base. Many rural communities in Kansas are faced with a continually declining economic base. The justification for a community's founding as an agricultural trade center, a manufacturing community, a location on transportation lines, or a center of natural resource extraction may no longer be valid for a variety of reasons.

As the base declines, or as farms and ranches get larger and more efficient so that fewer people are needed, the service sector of the economy takes on greater importance. This trend only leads to greater decline as young persons, not easily attracted to shops and banks where opportunity is limited, eventually leave for the city.

The economic base issue is clearly recognized by concerned citizens throughout the state of Kansas. One of the stated goals of the Greater Southwest Regional Planning Commission at Garden City, Kansas, is to develop ways to attract young people to stay or return to their communities and thus to stabilize the population by providing economic opportunity.

Population Change. As the population of the trade area declines, the central city of the region, which is often the county seat, either gains population or experiences very slight losses. Meanwhile, the small cities in the region often lose population to the point that they fail to exist as anything more than a small collection of houses near the elevator on a railroad siding. Communities such as Kanona and Speed in western Kansas are but two examples of this situation.

The change in the age composition of the population of rural communities also presents a significant problem. Many rural communities have a large elderly population that for the most part has not been integrated into community decision making by the leadership. Marysville, Kansas, a strong regional trade center, has over twenty percent of its population in the over 65 category, half of which is over 75.

Transportation and Communication Facilities. Although most of the regional trade and business centers have adequate access to transportation and communication facilities, many of the small towns are virtually ignored by business carriers. Public transportation is also missing except for school buses serving students and small buses for the elderly in some communities. Other citizens have nothing except automobiles and an occasional Greyhound or Continental bus.

Indifference to the Environment. The early communities in Kansas were located on rivers for transportation reasons. Hence, they were often built on active flood plains. Although flood control measures now prevent serious flooding in most Kansas communities, the attitude of "Don't fix anything up in this area because it might get damaged by high water" is still prevalent, particularly in business districts, the area most often seen by visitors and used by residents.

Many small communities do not have a city manager or anyone looking after routine maintenance or development issues. As a result junk is left strewn about the town, trash is not picked up regularly, curbs and gutters are not replaced, streets are not repaired, weeds grow in ditches, and dead trees are not removed. The citizens are generally indifferent to the environment. (Notice that nothing has been said about other more sophisticated and significant environmental issues such as historic preservation of old buildings and spaces.)

Leadership Void. There is perhaps not so much a leadership void as the problem of leaders whose personal interests and experiences cause decisions to be delayed, postponed, or forgotten. As one rural city commissioner noted, "We often adjourn in lieu of making a decision."

If the leaders of a community are over fifty years of age, they have the disadvantage of remembering the depression era of the 1930s. The dust storms, drought, and farm losses of this period were so catastrophic that the decision making of leaders in this age group is seriously affected, consciously or unconsciously. The lack of imagination that they are often criticized for may be a result of a conservative "tough it out" attitude brought on by their experiences in these tragic years.

Leadership in many rural communities is centralized, with the result that, even if the leader is liberal and progressive in outlook, he or she becomes the visible target for the opposition. A single leader in a community may find efforts to promote recreation programs opposed by persons who, though indifferent to recreation, have been angered by the leader's proposals and activities in downtown redevelopment. If the leader is also a banker, a professional, or a person of wealth, real or imagined, there is the foundation for thwarting almost any activity proposed by the centralized leadership.

Unfortunately, leaders in numerous communities choose to separate themselves from the citizens at large by participating in various organizations not open to the general public. The "elite status" antagonizes some persons and makes it possible for them to organize opposition to the decisions of community leaders.

Finally, the inactivity of the leadership is encouraged by a passive citizenry that does not demand creative decisions to changing situations.

Citizens of rural communities find it easy to be complacent, believing that they alone are participating in the good life. As they watch television, they see the crime and violence of the big city, the inhumanity of government agencies, the problems of management of big cities, and much more. Furthermore, the media tend to portray rural life as simple, direct, and worry free, for the most part ignoring such problems as rural poverty and isolation. Although it is easy to ignore rural problems, they exist; indeed, the illusion that they do not exist is perhaps the biggest problem of all.

Innovative approaches to rural problems are conspicuously absent from the modern planning literature on community development, although plentiful sources are available on case studies of the problems (i.e., the results of mall building and the delivery of social services).

Kansas has been involved in rural development for forty years with some success and some obvious and major failures. At the heart of the failures has always been the tendency to ignore the obvious—that every town cannot be developed, that industry is seldom the answer to rural needs, that governmental and political structures are weak and that the state is basically unwilling to intercede with workable programs and grants.

Kansas has several programs related to the planning and development of rural small towns and unincorporated areas. The Kansas PRIDE program (Programming Resources and Initiatives for Development Efforts) is one of the oldest state or private rural development efforts in the Midwest. The administration of this program is in the hands of a committee composed of, among others, the Kansas Department of Economic Development, the League of Kansas Municipalities, Kansas State University, the Kansas Gas and Electric Company, and the Union Pacific Railroad. Representatives of each organization meet regularly to establish goals, assess the current status of the program, and attend to routine administration.

The PRIDE program is open to any community in Kansas. When an application is made to the committee by a community, an initial commitment is made to enter into a planning and development process. The achievements of all communities are monitored throughout the year by the Kansas Department of Economic Development, and at the end of the year judges are selected statewide to decide which communities have made the greatest achievement in community development.

The PRIDE program, at least on paper, sounds very similar to any number of other community incentive projects throughout the nation. It is, however, non-traditional in the sense that it obligates all participating communities to a formal planning process that depends more upon local citizen participation than governmental decision making.

Early proponents of the PRIDE program had great difficulty in persuading professional planners and public administrators to participate or to take the program seriously. Over the years the annual awards and inter-community competition have generated such concrete results that statewide attention has been focused upon these local activities. The PRIDE program is essentially rural, non-metropolitan in orientation. It is predicated on a self-help attitude by local government; its focus is upon the maximum use of local resources.

Another approach, the Community Development Team, was initiated by the Kansas Department of Economic Development and was jointly funded by the state of Kansas, the Ozarks Regional Planning Commission, and the Economic Development Administration. The Community Development Team is a technical assistance group of private consultants, employed on a year to year basis by the state of Kansas and engaged in direct assistance to small communities.

The direct technical aid concept appears to be an essential ingredient to small town planning. Community officials and leaders in small towns have had little success in obtaining information and assistance from the states. The small town generally does not seek a planning program, but rather resolution of a number of serious problems.

The Community Development Team has been successful in putting together a program for obtaining and financing a community operated movie theater for one municipality; for another, it initiated a full trade area study and a continuing process of downtown improvement. The team assisted some communities by designing attitudinal surveys, for others, urban design concepts aimed at unifying center business districts. The program has so far produced highly visible results in the form of historic preservation, park and recreation plans, public facilities and a continuing planning process.

The Community Development Team approach is also essentially a program of local self help. The team assisted in organizing community committees for various activities before they conducted any business with a community. The approach is more closely tied to local government than is the PRIDE program, but the concept of community development is predicated upon the development of local resources rather than upon state or federal grants.

A third approach, metropolitan planning, is conducted by the city of Wichita through their Metropolitan Area Planning Department. This city-county regional planning agency works with all local communities within Sedgwick County and assists in the preparation of local policies, plans and ordinances. It is not a technical assistance program in the sense of PRIDE or the Community Development Team.

Finally, the Mini-Plan concept is a development of the Center for Regional and Community Planning at Kansas State University and the Kansas Department of Economic Development. The Mini-Plan is a technical manual and aid for the preparation of comprehensive plans in small communities. Like the previous community development programs, the Mini-Plan seeks to utilize local resources in the preparation and assessment of the comprehensive plan. Professionals are used only for review and for the preparation of some projections and forecasts. The few communities that have prepared the Mini-Plan have benefited substantially. Very little additional assistance in the local community has been needed after the community has spent from one to two years in the drafting of this document.

Prior to the formation of Regional Planning Agencies in Kansas, rural communities had little, if any, access to organizations which could help them with planning and management assistance of a comprehensive nature. If the communities could identify their problems, they could always retain good planning consultants. Now, the comprehensive look at community problems is provided by staff members of the regional planning agency who assist communities in dealing with technical problems of a general nature, help complete application for a variety of federal grants, and identify projects that can be undertaken by professional planning consultants. For example, one small Kansas community worked with its Regional Planning Agency to determine the assets and the liabilities of the community. The agency then assisted them in the preparation of applications for specific federal grants that related to the kinds of activities the community could support and the kinds of facilities needed. The community was thus in a position to work effectively with the planning, architectural, and engineering consultants who developed detailed plans for effectively using a $600,000 grant.

Much of the technical assistance currently focuses on health care, programs for the elderly, criminal justice, drug abuse, recreation, water and sewer, and housing programs. Other efforts are directed toward assisting communities with planning, zoning, subdivision, and capital improvement strategies.

The Regional Planning Agencies in Kansas have, thus far, been creative in developing local programs. They have a stronger relationship to local government than do regional agencies in many other states because they were organized by cautious community leaders and citizen groups who first weighed the advantages and disadvantages of regional planning against their concern for saving the taxpayers' money and then committed themselves to planning, deciding that it was not only important but vital. Once these leaders made this decision, they communicated with fellow citizens. One local organizer said that he presented the pros and cons of regional planning at over 300 meetings to city commissions, county commissions, church organizations, citizen groups and service organizations. He kept at it until they understood the issues involved in regional planning and were willing to see local tax dollars used to support the activity. As a result, the regional planning agencies have strong local support and they, in turn, are successful in identifying programs which are meaningful to their regions. Two samples of their creativity are the roving city manager program of the Chikaskia-Indian Hills-Golden Belt Regional Planning Commission and the Home Insulation program for rural farm homes of the Big Lakes Regional Planning Commission.

The state of Kansas has rarely provided assistance of a comprehensive nature in planning and management to rural communities except in specific topic areas. For example, the State Department of Transportation is very thorough; however, until recently all its attention was focused on the design and development of highways. Now they are working on studies concerning a variety of issues, including land use, involved in transportation decisions. However, they do not integrate their studies with the detailed, comprehensive plans of a community except in a general way. Fortunately, the Department of Transportation and other state agencies now rely on the local regional planning agencies to integrate state studies with local planning and management strategies.

Another agency, the Kansas Department of Economic Development, has provided extensive assistance to local groups in the organization of regional planning commissions, but it has not helped any of these agencies develop planning and management strategies.

Prior to the formation of the regional planning agencies, much of the technical assistance provided to local communities came from the academic departments of the universities in Kansas and from the Cooperative Extension Service at Kansas State University. This assistance was helpful but was generally not as effective as it should have been, for the universities could not afford to pay persons to aid communities distant from the campus.

Perhaps the most effective programs have been short courses and general educational programs in community planning and management presented in communities throughout the state by various academic departments and the Cooperative Extension Service.

Kansans looking for ways to plan and develop their rural communities must continue to look to themselves for ideas and inspiration to accomplish community development goals. With the formation and expansion of regional planning commission staffs, they may continue to get creative technical assistance when they ask for it. But unfortunately, the regional planning commission staff in Kansas is not large enough to contact all local planning units in a region to make them aware of development and management potentials.

The various programs described in this paper, including the PRIDE program, mini-plan program, university assistance programs, and so on, have the potential for providing rural areas with the incentive to plan and manage. None of these programs are formally coordinated, although the personnel in charge of various programs are generally cooperative persons who work well together when the opportunity is present.

Kansans generally are distrustful of state government agencies. As a result, the planning and management activities which have been developed locally are often ones that the various state agencies have had little to do with. Furthermore, the locally developed programs, technically assisted by the regional planning agencies, often have strong support just because they were organized locally. Local involvement, by necessity, may be the strongest element in rural planning in Kansas.

NOTES

[1] The Homestead Laws include a large number of acts and amendments passed by Congress over a period of fifty to sixty years. The most well known provisions of these laws can be found in Sections 2289–2312 of the *Revised Statutes of the United States*.

[2] By resourcefulness and a little planning, an individual could homestead considerably more than 160 acres. Additional land could be bought under Timber Acts, Stone Acts, and the Desert Land Acts.

[3] Paul Gates, *Fifty Million Acres: Conflicts Over Kansas Land Policy: 1854-1890* (Ithaca, N.Y.: Cornell Univ. Press, 1954), pp. 251–52.

Continuity and Change in a
Small Southern Town

CHARLES A. CLINTON

The issues of continuity and change in small American towns have interested social scientists for the last five decades. From those interests have emerged two major orientations for facilitating change in local communities. The first may be termed the impact model,[1] in which decisions made in the centers of power produce predictable changes in local units.[2] The second may be termed the local autonomy model, in which local decisions, and the reasons for them, are more powerful tools for predicting the courses of continuity and change in the American small town than are decisions made in the centers of power.[3] This paper tests both orientations and concludes with the suggestion that an external agency might well consider the implications of the test before attempting to facilitate either continuity or change in an American small town.

The data were gathered during three and one half years of fieldwork in Shiloh County, a pseudonym for a rural political subdivision of the American South.[4] Shiloh contains two small towns, Cuba Landing and Clarksville. Cuba Landing had a 1960 population of 610 while Clarksville showed 882 residents in the 1960 census. A political entity, the Shiloh County Planning and Zoning Commission, holds the legal right to police land use in the towns and the larger community areas served by them. The story of the commission and its effectiveness tests the impact model.

Shiloh's Planning and Zoning Commission was formed because Cuba Landing and Clarksville discharged raw sewage into public waterways. The Environmental Protection Agency informed the towns that further discharge was illegal and that funds were available to construct sewage treatment plants, provided that Cuba Landing and Clarksville made joint application and that both towns, along with the Shiloh County Fiscal Court, agreed to participate in land use planning.

The bargain was struck. The towns received funds to build sewage treatment plants and Shiloh County had a new Planning and Zoning Commission. The commission's public mandate was to insure that desirable development took place. The commission's private mandate was not to harass Shiloh's residents. The private mandate assumed priority for three reasons: (1) local governments appointed commission members; (2) all three local governments could override zoning decisions, a fact the commission's chairman stressed in a visit to the Clarksville City Council—"The planning and zoning commission is purely an advisory group. Any rezoning we have done, you can overrule. It is really up to the city council to vote to approve or disapprove the rulings"; and (3) local governments supplied the commission's budget.

These three checks on the commission's power insured that the federal policy of policing land use had only a minimal to imaginary impact in Shiloh County. Consider, for example, the following imaginable scenario. Two local men asked the commission to approve a subdivision plat. Their request was denied—zoning regulations called for paved roads and the plat showed gravel roads.

The developers asked Fiscal Court to override the commission's ruling. A magistrate objected, "We're setting precedent. We're not just deciding one case. We're going to have to live with this from now on." Mr. Bass, Shiloh's County Judge, demurred. "Way I see it, we're setting precedent. But we want the county to grow, don't we?"

The Fiscal Court overruled the commission and the subdivision was developed despite zoning rules to the contrary. Public and private interests seemed suspiciously to have entered into the court's decision. The court could publicly overturn the commission's ruling on grounds that "the subdivision helped Shiloh's growth." Judge Bass's advocacy for development was based on his personal political reckonings—he was in a campaign for reelection. One developer was active in the Judge's political party, while the other was influential in the news coverage of the election campaign. Judge Bass could not afford to alienate either man.

Giving greater weight to local factors than to federal priorities characterized all commission decisions. When the commission learned that a congregation was building a church in violation of zoning rules, the chairman recognized the power of religion in Shiloh and quelled debate with, "I don't want to be facetious, but I'm not going to take on either the church or God." There the matter ended.

Commission members said that local factors should be more important than federal priorities, that the commission's rules were created by a nationally known research firm unfamiliar with Shiloh, and that its recommendations, which were based on these rules, were thus in need of correction. As one alienated commission member said of development in Clarksville, "To hamper the growth of a town because of a map that is arbitrarily set up—that's ridiculous."

Shiloh's citizens agreed with the alienated commission member. One citizen was present when the chairman of the commission approached the Clarksville City Council with a budget request. The citizen said, "I've been opposed to this thing from its very inception. This ordinance was brought about because the federal government told Clarksville and Cuba Landing "no" on some grants unless we had a planning and zoning commission. The people of Shiloh County cannot live with this thing." (Unless, of course, this "thing" was responsive to local priorities rather than federal policy.) Since the commission's decisions were routinely refashioned in local political arenas, the federal land use program that depended on the commission's workings had little impact on the county.

The workings of the Shiloh Planning and Zoning Commission suggest that local factors can stay the outcomes of federal programs. To extend the scenario further, one can envision the local factors that induce both continuity and change. What follows is the case of the Shiloh County Courthouse.

The Shiloh County Courthouse was built in Clarksville in the late 1860s. Between 1870 and 1900 the county's economy and population grew and the courthouse was maintained. But the twentieth century brought economic and demographic declines to Shiloh. By 1960 the county's fortunes were at low ebb, and the courthouse, the symbolic center of a Southern county,[5] epitomized the deterioration. What was once an exemplar of Federalist architecture was now a decrepit building.

The county's citizens sought ways to reverse Shiloh's fortune, and Cuba Landing found a way to do so. In 1963 Cuba Landing joined with other small towns and successfully lobbied the state legislature to allow small political subdivisions to issue Municipal Industrial Bonds. Cuba Landing immediately issued $50 million worth of bonds to construct a metals processing plant near the town. Initial industrialization was followed by the construction of an electrical generating plant, an integrated pulp and paper unit, and a complex of metal processing and fabrication plants built with the proceeds of a $150 million Shiloh County Fiscal Court Municipal Bond Issuance. In five years, from 1963 to 1968, this agricultural county induced nearly $300 million worth of industrial facilities to locate within its boundaries.

But Shiloh's growth created a problem: the new plants did not spark an expansion of local business or governmental undertakings because seventy percent of the work force lived outside the county and because the plants built with the proceeds of Municipal Industrial Bonds were the nominal property of local governments and thus not included on local property tax rolls. Shiloh had found ways to transform its economy only to discover that rural industrialization does not lead to rural development.[6]

Then the legal system changed in Shiloh's favor. The State Constitution had assigned all powers not specifically granted to individual political subdivisions to the state. In 1971 the state legislature passed a bill giving local political subdivisions all powers not specifically reserved for state or federal governments. Local political subdivisions now had the right to levy a tax on payrolls disbursed within their boundaries.

The right to tax industrial payrolls, and thus convert commuting workers into a base for funding public undertakings, split Shiloh's body politic into two factions. The proponents consisted of businessmen, town politicians, and some members of the Fiscal Court. The President of Shiloh's Chamber of Commerce phrased the pro position as, "We provide jobs, but we are unable to provide services" because of budget constraints. The con faction consisted of wage earners and small farmers. A member of this group expressed the opposition position with, "I'll take care of myself. Why can't everybody else?"

The Fiscal Court scheduled public meetings to discuss both the imposition of the tax and Shiloh's priorities, including the state of the courthouse. The argument in favor of the tax was stated in blunt economic terms by the magistrate from Clarksville. "This is the cheapest way to get the money. If it doesn't happen this way, it's going to have to be done another."

The public meetings produced no clear mandate, but they did produce a political lever. Mr. Bass, Shiloh's county judge, was in an election campaign. When asked to state his constituents' preferences about the tax, Judge Bass said, "Of all the people I've talked with, the majority were either for or against it." Local analysis said Judge Bass was waffling because the payroll tax was controversial and any action on it would have consequences among Shiloh's voters.

Judge Bass's problems were magnified by a consensus among the other four members of the Fiscal Court. The magistrates were opposed to Judge Bass's reelection and determined to use the payroll tax to defeat him. At the next regular session of the Fiscal Court, the Clarksville magistrate moved to impose a one percent payroll tax. The magistrate from Cuba Landing seconded the motion. The magistrates from Cuba Landing and Clarksville voted for the motion, the magistrates from Shiloh's rural areas abstained. Judge Bass would have to cast the third and deciding ballot and reap the political consequences at the polls.

The tax passed by a vote of three to nothing and Judge Bass lost the election to Mr. Henry. Judge Henry came into office with new funding with which to address Shiloh County's priorities, including the courthouse. Judge Henry approached the courthouse with a mixture of private and political agenda. Privately he was in favor of restoring the courthouse. Politically he weighed the decision against his ambitions for higher office. The people he turned to for advice convinced him that the greatest political advantage was in restoring a historical landmark to its original appearance. Judge Henry accepted this counsel and made the restoration of the courthouse a goal of his administration.

Judge Henry's goal was not completely congruent with his Fiscal Court's internal political agenda. The magistrates from Clarksville and Cuba Landing wanted to use payroll tax money to replace the courthouse with a modern structure. The magistrates from Shiloh's rural areas wanted to do nothing with the courthouse and use payroll tax monies to pave roads in their districts. To achieve his goal, Judge Henry had to find ways of reconciling, or at least pacifying, the conflicting factions.

A minor federal program seemed to give Judge Henry the option of gaining his goal. The Department of Housing and Urban Development set aside eight million dollars to help the state's rural counties and towns improve blighted areas and restore historic buildings. "We can get one hundred percent money for the historic preservation of this building. You can't get any of this money to build a new courthouse. It's for anything you want to restore to its original appearances," Judge Henry explained to the court.

"It's crazy. The federal government is crazy," said a court member opposed to restoring the courthouse.

The court held a public meeting to inform people of the opportunity. Judge Henry told those attending that he had taken part in a seminar sponsored by the Department of Housing and Urban Development. "I'm hopeful that what I found out will have some effect on the court's decision. HUD set certain guidelines on how this money may be spent. And when you read the guidelines, you think someone must have been thinking of Shiloh County. I'd like to be authorized to seek out this commercial development money. It will cost absolutely nothing to try."

"Let's go get it," said a magistrate from one of Shiloh's rural areas, and the court authorized Judge Henry to begin the application process.

The initial application met with success. The state representative of the Department of Housing and Urban Development said, "This is one of the four best applications I've looked at." He went on to advise Judge Henry to file a joint application with the City of Clarksville.

Judge Henry met with the Clarksville City Council to explain the Fiscal Court's application and to stress the need for cooperation: "I'm coming here tonight with my hat in my hand. Shiloh County needs the support of the Clarksville City Council. In order to make this thing work, we need a joint proposal. The federal government and the state government want to see local governments work together. I'm here tonight to tell you we need you. We need you in the worst way."

"How much is this going to cost?" asked the Clarksville City Attorney.

"It won't cost the city of Clarksville anything," said Judge Henry.

"I'm in favor of the joint application," said the mayor of Clarksville.

"It'll do more for Clarksville than any little thing we can do," said a councilman. The rest of the council agreed and the motion was made, seconded, and passed to file a joint application.

The joint application was filed, but met with no success in Washington. Judge Henry's hope of using external funds to finesse the court's internal disagreements over spending priorities was over. The Judge was now obliged to deal with the conflicting priorities of the court to gain a three vote majority. He soon learned that a coalition depended on his support for paved roads in rural Shiloh.

The strength of the coalition first appeared in a special called meeting of the Fiscal Court to inform the public about the courthouse. The magistrates from Clarksville and Cuba Landing wanted to replace the building and used costs to justify their decision. A new building would cost about a million dollars. Renovation and construction of an annex would cost about one and one half million. The magistrates from rural Shiloh rejected costs as a basis for decision making. "My mind is made up. The figures don't do much for me," said a magistrate from a rural district.

The Clarksville magistrate then moved to tear down the courthouse and replace it with a new structure. The Cuba Landing magistrate seconded. The County Clerk called for the vote. Clarksville and Cuba Landing were in favor. The two magistrates from rural Shiloh were opposed. Judge Henry abstained. There were no further motions.

The members of the Fiscal Court discussed the courthouse for a month. The discussions led no one to alter his position. The court also received counsel from outside. Judge Henry was publicly told by the President of the Chamber of Commerce that, while the Chamber did not wish to dictate solutions, it wanted a decision. Judge Henry summarized the attitude of the Fiscal Court at the beginning of a second special called meeting: "I think it's important before we leave here tonight that we come to a final decision."

"I want to save this building," said a magistrate from rural Shiloh.

"It looks like the cards are on the table. We're split. I'd just like for us to do something. Right or wrong," said the Clarksville magistrate.

"What's the feeling of the court?" asked Judge Henry.

"I'll make a motion to preserve this building and go across the street to build an annex," said a magistrate from rural Shiloh. The second magistrate from rural Shiloh seconded the motion. The vote was taken. The magistrates from rural Shiloh were in favor. The magistrates from Clarksville and Cuba Landing were opposed. Judge Henry cast the final ballot in favor. The court opted for continuity in keeping the old courthouse, but also opted for change in its decision to restore the structure and to build an annex.

This essay began by noting that fifty years of social scientific interest in the issues of continuity and change in small American towns has led to two major orientations among those who wish to facilitate change. One orientation coalesces around the impact model, the other around the local autonomy model. The purpose of this essay was to test both orientations to see which is the most powerful approach for inducing either continuity or change in small towns.

The data from Shiloh County denies the impact orientation. The Federal government's attempt to create a local agency with police powers over land use failed because local interests found ways of making the Planning and Zoning Commission responsive to local priorities. This finding is neither unusual nor remarkable. In a major review of the Federal budget, a team of economists concluded that federal approaches to change, which are structured by the impact model, "are not particularly effective."[7] This domestic insight was seconded by an interdisciplinary group of social scientists who surveyed international efforts at facilitating planned change and decided that the impact orientation was "if not irrelevant, then less relevant as a model" than what they called "development from below," an approach that looks to local factors to explain both the successes and failures of change programs.[8]

Shiloh County is an exemplar of development from below. The cases of the Planning and Zoning Commission, Municipal Industrial Bonding, industrialization, the imposition of a payroll tax, and the courthouse all show a set of small local units choosing futures compatible with local priorities. Again, this finding is neither unusual nor remarkable. The team of budget analysts who found Federal approaches to inducing change ineffective also concluded that the successes and failures of federal programs depend on how well they are "adapted to local conditions."[9]

The foregoing scenarios and conclusions reveal some limits in the role of agencies external to small towns. Before committing to ventures for inducing either continuity or change, external agencies, such as the Center for Small Town Research and Design at Mississippi State University, might do well to consider local conditions and priorities—for the exercise of local autonomy may well determine the success or failure of policies and programs.

NOTES

[1]John Bennett, "Microcosm-Macrocosm Relationships in North American Agrarian Society," *American Anthropologist,* 69 (1967), 442.

[2]Arthur J. Vidich and Joseph Bensman, *Small Town in Mass Society: Class, Power, and Religion in a Rural Community,* rev. ed., (Princeton, N.J.: Princeton Univ. Press, 1968), pp. 386–87.

[3]Bennett, p. 442.

[4]Carole E. Hill, "Anthropological Studies in the American South: Review and Directions," *Current Anthropology,* 18 (1977), 309.

[5]Conrad M. Arensberg and Solon T. Kimball, *Culture and Community* (New York: Harcourt, Brace, and World, 1965), pp. 106–07.

[6]Gene F. Summers, "Small Towns Beware: Industry Can Be Costly," *Planning,* 42 (1976), 20–21.

[7]Charles L. Schultze, Edward R. Fried, Alice M. Rivlin, and Nancy H. Teeters, *Setting National Priorities: The 1973 Budget* (Washington, D. C.: Brookings Institution, 1972), p. 458.

[8]David C. Pitt, "Introduction," in *Development From Below: Anthropologists And Developmental Situations,* ed. David C. Pitt (The Hague: Mouton, 1976), p. 4.

[9]Schultze, et al., p. 453.

Introduction to
Technology and Town Form

ARNOLD J. AHO

The degree of impact of technology on the form of the small town has fluctuated throughout Western history. These variances appear to have both cultural and temporal dimensions worth considering.

With the end of the Middle Ages and the advent of the Renaissance there was an emergence of fortified towns from highly organic medieval villages. These ideal cities ("Citta' Ideale") by such designers as Filarete (1400–1469), DiGiorgio (1439–1502) and DaVinci (1452–1519), revealed not only a fascination for geometric order, but a distinctly applied technology. For example, based on military armaments and strategies, the walls of these star-shaped cities were studded with wedge-like bastions carefully engineered to enable defenders to rake the ranks of attacking forces from whatever direction they approached. Likewise, the radiating street pattern also enabled rapid troop deployments to beleaguered points from a central command position. In *Space, Time and Architecture,* Sigfried Giedion maintains that with the breakdown of the principle of self-government that characterized the Renaissance, "It was clear that these star-shaped towns were principally meant to serve as fortresses."[1]

Military considerations naturally were not the only technological influences on town form. With the settlement of America there were direct correlations between energy exploitation and the siting and organization of inland settlements. Early mill towns were located where river gradients permitted the extraction of energy by water wheels and turbines. As the industrial revolution gained momentum, these early mill towns expanded along the sources of water power and eventually developed into remarkably-scaled early industrial cities such as Lowell, Massachusetts, and Manchester, New Hampshire.

71

The advent of the railroads with their concurrent technologies had an equally dramatic impact on the forms of midwest and prairie towns during the last century.

While the preceding examples illustrate only a few of the diverse ways in which technology has influenced town forms, there does seem to emerge a common factor: the *degree of necessity* of technology to the survival of the town itself, whether a response to military defense or to the need for power to sustain a life-blood industry.

There have been other periods in western history, however, when technology has been less critical, or has been overridden by socio-cultural factors. Very possibly the actual success of technology diminishes its own impact on town form. Amos Rapoport, in *House Form and Culture,* suggests that: "Our era is one of reduced physical constraints. [Thanks to technology] we can do very much more than was possible in the past, and criticality is lower than ever. The result is the problem of excessive choice, the difficulty of selecting or finding constraints which arose naturally in the past and which are necessary for the creation of meaningful house form."[2]

It seems to be the greatest paradox of our time that while we believe we live in the age of technology and materialism, these appear to have little impact on the form of our towns and cities. Alan Watts, the American philosopher, has observed:

> . . . it strikes me more and more that America's reputation for materialism is unfounded—that is—if a materialist is a person who thoroughly enjoys the physical world and loves material things. In this sense we are superb materialists when it comes to the construction of jet aircraft, but when we decorate the inside of these magnificent monsters for the comfort of passengers, it is nothing but frippery: high-heeled, narrow-hipped, doll-like girls serving imitation, warmed-over meals. For our pleasures are not material pleasures, but *symbols* of pleasure—attractively packaged, but inferior in content . . . [made of] a mixture of plaster-of-paris, paper maché, and plastic glue.[3]

Much of this description holds true for the current images of our towns and cities. The houses built today imitate forms that evolved two or three hundred years earlier in colonial America, while vinyl siding and aluminum windows have replaced the brick and wood of the past. Our commercial and industrial buildings apply "image" to their shells by bolting on prefabricated mansard roof facades. With the possible exception of our new highway systems, technology not only has had seemingly little direct influence on the image of the present built environment: more often than not it has been called upon to take part in this chicanery of shapes. As Alan Watts has written, "Building materials abound in both quantity and variety, yet most homes look as if they had been made by someone who had heard of a house, but never seen one."[4]

These comments are not intended, however to be a prophesy of "gloom-and-doom" for the future image of the small town. If, indeed, the influence of technology increases with the degree of criticality, it has a survival role to fulfill in the future. The global issues of environmental quality, depletion of natural resources, and energy promise to challenge our entire way of life, and technology will be called upon for essential responses.

Significantly, the two papers that follow concern primarily the implementation of technological and design concerns in the small town. It is through this facilitation, or acceptance, of technology that the order and image of the small town will change.

NOTES

[1]Sigfried Giedion, *Space, Time and Architecture* (Harvard Univ. Press, 1963), pp. 52–53.

[2]Amos Rapoport, *House Form and Culture* (Prentice-Hall, 1969), p. 135.

[3]Alan Watts, *The Book; On the Taboo Against Knowing Who You Are* (New York: Vintage, 1972), p. 76.

[4]Watts, p. 75.

Strategies for Energy
Conservation in Small Towns

MICHAEL J. BUONO

The ongoing energy crisis has affected the total American society more than any other circumstance since World War II. It has already had a limited effect on American lifestyle and will have a much greater effect in the years to come. With the energy situation have come many related economic problems. The rising prices of crude oil and natural gas have caused double-digit inflation, increasing the costs of food, shelter, and virtually every other commodity.

The energy crisis is threatening the future of the small town. The desired new prosperity, the economic boom that was to come from the exodus of people from cities in search of a better quality of life, may become mired in the ever worsening energy crisis.

Because of their compactness, urban areas have certain economies and advantages in terms of energy. Denser environments reduce travel distance from point to point, making mass transit feasible, and denser, attached housing requires less fuel for heating and cooling.

The small town of today does not benefit from the advantages of density. The majority of housing is single-family detached, and the distance between dwelling and services is greater than in cities. The private automobile is the major means of transit. Utilities such as gas or electricity are generally supplied by companies in larger towns, and because delivery distances are greater, the cost is higher to the small-town resident than to the urban resident. Contrary to what most people believe, certain food commodities in small towns may also cost more, chiefly because of the distance trucks have to travel to deliver them and the absence of economies available in retail food stores purchasing larger volumes.

As the supply of energy in any form diminishes and the cost of it rises, small towns will be affected more and more. Small towns cannot do very much to solve the crisis nationally, but they can act locally. Ultimately, decisions to take action at the local level may mean the difference between the survival or destruction of the small town. Some excellent innovative strategies for meeting the crisis have been suggested by Bill Kopper and David Bainbridge in "Energy Conservation for Small Towns,"[1] which I have drawn on frequently in the following discussion.

Design Strategies

The first thing a small town will have to do to achieve a considerably high level of success in energy conservation is to organize a governmental body or a group of concerned citizens, or both, willing to work to conserve energy. This group would be responsible for identifying and researching general and specific energy concerns and for the developing and coordinating of an overall Comprehensive Energy Conservation Program for the town.

Within the group the town can set up an energy task force and appoint one person as the energy coordinator with overall responsibility. This person might be hired in this capacity full time; or, if the budget is tight, the job could be handled on a part-time basis by someone already on local government staff. In many cases the task force may not have the expertise necessary to develop the appropriate program standards and guidelines. In these cases, when necessary, state universities and state energy offices could help by providing either expertise or funds to acquire expertise.

The first major step the task force might take is the adoption of a new Energy Conservation Building Code for the town that is appropriate to its climate. Detailed climatic data on maximum and minimum temperatures, precipitation, wind, humidity, cloudiness, radiation and information on desired comfort levels in buildings can be used to set up building standards so that buildings will mitigate the external climatic conditions and achieve the desired comfort levels with the lowest possible use of energy for heating and cooling. Once standards are decided upon, design guidelines should be developed to allow architects and builders to meet the standards. These guidelines could include recommendations on such items as insulation standards, building orientation, site planning, zoning of interior and exterior functions, light-colored roofs, thermopane insulated glass, the use of thermal mass and the shading of glass areas.

In particular, all new buildings should be constructed with adequate insulation to achieve optimum insulation values for heating and cooling. Recommended R values, which vary depending on climate zone, are set for the South at R-26 for ceilings, R-19 for walls and R-13 for floors.

When siting and designing a dwelling in the hot-humid Southeastern zone of the U.S., movement of air through the site and shade are very important. Outdoor living areas should be on the north or east of the house and both the outdoor living areas and the house should be shaded by plantings. A paved and protected winter sun pocket may be created as an outdoor patio for winter use. Wind funnels should be created with walls, shrubs and hedges to direct breezes through the house and outdoor living areas.[2]

The buildings should be designed to capture prevailing breezes in the summer for natural cooling and ventilation. In hot, humid areas elevating the house to allow air movement beneath it reduces both heat and humidity. The day of the fixed window should be gone with buildings making use of well insulated, operable windows for natural cooling. Roofing materials should be light colored to reduce absorption of the high summer sun's rays.

The climate in the South is generally favorable for natural heating. Many sunny winter days allow the use of passive and active solar heating and solar hot water heating in buildings, particularly residences. New residences should be oriented with their long sides east-west and have large areas of glass to the South backed by adequate thermal mass to store the low-angle winter sunlight. Heavy, durable, folding and sliding insulation barriers should be utilized on the interior to cover glass areas at night to reduce heat loss.

A building that is sited, landscaped, and designed in such a way that it buffers the cold winds from the north and northeast and has minimum openings to these sides will require less fuel to heat than one with large expanses of glass or door openings on these orientations. In the case of residences, these sides may contain storage facilities, closets, workshops and sleeping areas. Daytime activity spaces, such as living, dining and cooking, could be on the east and south sides, which can benefit from the warmth of the sun in the winter.[3] South and west facing windows of these areas should have overhangs or deciduous trees to block the summer sun and eliminate direct heat gain.

Such design considerations would form the Energy Conservation Building Code. Once the code is completed and ready for adoption, the energy task force may find that passage by the city council and acceptance by local architects, developers and builders will come more readily if they are shown that any additional building costs can be recouped within a short time through utility bill savings.

Retrofitting Existing Buildings

The comprehensive energy program must also include existing dwellings. New energy building codes generally are for new construction and do not affect the existing houses that make up a large part of small towns. To save energy in these homes requires a retrofit program. Ordinarily, the easiest and cheapest way of retrofitting is weatherstripping doors and windows and insulating walls and floors, particularly on many houses that are raised on piers.

Also worth considering are ventilating attic spaces, adding vestibules or entry halls to reduce infiltration of outside air when opening or closing doors, adding a greenhouse to serve as a passive solar collector and control heat transfer, and installing operable window shutters or heavy curtains to keep out the sun in summer and the heat in during the winter. Window solar box collectors and window-box greenhouses, as well as the installation of an efficient wood burning stove, are also good retrofitting measures for existing homes. To encourage the residents who live in existing dwellings to participate in retrofitting their homes, a tax break at all levels should be given for any energy conservation remodeling. Free assistance and consultation should be provided by state and local agencies.

Planning Strategies

Land use and transportation planning decisions are very significant for small towns because they affect the transportation patterns, the growth, the environmental quality and the consumption of energy.

Within the Comprehensive Energy Conservation Program a planning program should be developed with policies that will eliminate wasteful habits resulting from current trends and patterns of land use and transportation. This program might stress the following policies:

Minimize Lot Size. Town planning policies that encourage large lots promote sprawl, increased service and utility distribution lines, paved areas, and consequently summer heating problems. Building lots should be of minimum size allowing adequate privacy, solar access and flexibility in setback regulations.[4]

Minimize Travel Distance. The trend of the past 25 years of separating the individual house by great distances from work, shopping facilities and schools has dictated physical dependency on the automobile. Policies should be adopted that place work and shopping areas, schools, and recreational facilities within a fifteen minute walking distance of residential sections.

Return to the Downtown. In many small towns the once thriving downtown is losing business to the extended vehicular-oriented bypass strip. These strips are visually chaotic: they increase gasoline consumption and reduce social interraction of the town's residents. A special zoning ordinance might be set up that would specify what types of commercial functions are permitted downtown and on the strip bypass. For example, plant nurseries and used car dealers may be the type of businesses located on the strip. Places which people frequent often, such as restaurants and food shops, would be downtown, reducing gasoline consumption and increasing social interraction.

Street System and Orientation. When planning a new small town or expanding an existing one, the layout and orientation of the street system can have an impact on energy conservation. In residential areas, the closing of certain intersections and streets can eliminate through traffic and slow down all traffic, making the streets safer and saving gasoline. The street system and building lots may also be oriented so that buildings take maximum advantage of the sun and the summer breezes.

Street Widths. Because of the increase in the use of the automobile, many small towns are widening their existing streets and building new ones wider than ever, even at a time when the widths of new cars are decreasing each year. Small towns should propose new street width standards which dictate a return to narrower streets. Research has shown that neighborhoods with wide unshaded streets are 10 degrees warmer in the summer than ones with narrower shaded streets. This 10 degrees more of heat outside requires approximately 50 percent more electricity for cooling inside buildings. Narrower streets also slow down traffic and are safer for motorists, bicyclists and pedestrians.

Landscaping. One of the beautiful qualities of small towns, particularly in the South, is landscaping. However, it is being lost in many communities. The lovely old trees that line the streets and surround the houses not only provide beauty but cooling shade. Such large deciduous trees as oaks, pecans, maples, hickories, and hackberries provide cooling shade and transpiration in the summer, and also shed their leaves in the winter and allow the warm sun to shine through.

Landscaping and shading may often be the determining factors when someone considers walking or bicycling in the summer or riding in an air-conditioned automobile. Hot, glaring, unshaded asphalt streets, parking lots and concrete sidewalks are not comfortable environments for pedestrians and cyclists. A good planning program should have ordinances and codes which encourage landscaping of new and existing building sites and the shading of streets and parking areas.

Transportation. Approximately 37.5 percent of the energy consumed in the predominantly rural state of Mississippi is used for transportation. As the supply of gasoline dwindles and the costs increase, people will have to turn to other forms of transportation. Small towns, because of their size and somewhat less hectic lifestyle, offer opportunities to look at alternative forms of transportation, particularly bicycling and walking. As distances between places are decreased, as previously proposed, walking and bicycling could be a pleasant experience, particularly if pedestrian and bike routes were well designed. Such changes encourage public social interaction and neighborliness, both of which are part of the small town tradition.

It will not be an easy task to convince people to reduce their use of automobiles for local travel. One system of transportation that might succeed is the TIP (Transport Individual Public) system, a system developed in France in 1971 using co-operatively owned automobiles. It was developed to promote the use of an automobile by several operators, and avoids having a vehicle sit unused in a garage, a parking lot or on the street. It has the further result of reducing the number of vehicles on the road, as each individual operator does not need one.[5]

The people of the town might form a cooperative and purchase a few specially equipped, low-consumption gas vehicles. The vehicles could be operated by members who insert a plastic disc, purchased locally, into a special metering device. Each disc would permit the vehicle to travel a certain number of miles within the town. Members would be able to gain entry into any TIP vehicle anywhere they find it and leave it at any designated lot when their trip is completed. This system would allow each TIP vehicle to replace fifteen to twenty privately owned cars. If successful, this system would bring about increased mobility of small town residents who cannot afford to own private automobiles, elimination of a second car in most small town families, provision of cheap local service with minor inconvenience relative to other forms of transportation, reduction in gas consumption and pollution, visual improvement of the environment, and an increase in money available to a family to use for other necessities.[6]

Self-Sufficiency Strategies

A final direction that small town residents should pursue is the development of renewed attitudes of conservation, self sufficiency, and use of local energy systems which were once part of the small town tradition. If towns do not develop these attitudes, if they continue the many unnecessary and wasteful habits that consume our resources, and if dilemmas recur such as the oil embargo or the truckers strike, we may not be able to count on a permanent supply of energy, food, and control of the forces that produce them. The question may ultimately become one of survival!

A variety of measures may be taken, such as local diversified food production, both at the community and individual level. In farming communities, animal waste can be used to produce methane for various uses. All future building can be designed to maximize solar energy and the forces of the wind can be captured to cool buildings in the summer as well as drive windmills to produce electricity.

Because of the abundance of wood and its renewability, the use of efficient wood burning stoves can be a big help in home heating. Efficient waste handling should begin at home with the separation of organic matter for composting and non-organic waste for recycling. Composting toilets such as the Clivus Multrum could be encouraged, replacing the current, water-wasting toilets. Community and individual water should be collected and stored for use in periods of short supply. "Grey water," such as that from bathing, should be used for irrigation.

The use of locally available materials in construction will reduce the necessity to move goods long distances and consequently will reduce the cost. Besides saving energy and money, the town will have a character that is indigenous to the area.

In order for the energy conservation program to succeed, it will be necessary to persuade the citizens of the community of the need for such a program and to show them the methods available for energy conservation. One way of accomplishing this persuasion is through an educational program organized by the energy task force and supported and conducted by various local groups such as the Elks club, church clubs, and the public utility companies. Once again, state and federal energy offices as well as the universities can help out by conducting seminars on conservation topics. The educational program will have to function at different levels—for elementary and secondary schools and for adults. There should also be a program set up to educate architects, developers, builders and building inspectors on how to work within the program and how to use the building codes and planning ordinances.

It will not be an easy task to adopt a comprehensive energy program that includes an Energy Conserving Building Code and planning policies. It depends on the willingness of elected officials and concerned citizen volunteers to put the program together, stand up against skeptical builders, developers, architects and citizens with status quo attitudes.

These ideas are not totally new. Many of them have been tried by the town of Davis, a community of about 30,000 near Sacramento, California. Citizens there have become aware of methods of energy conservation and have reduced their electricity consumption by ten percent in a short period of three years. By adopting an Energy Conserving Building Code the new houses being built save about fifty percent of the energy needed for heating and cooling. Townspeople have also developed such planning policies as narrowing streets, planting shade trees, developing additional pedestrian and bicycle routes, and protecting solar rights. Davis demonstrates that a small town may have a substantial impact on its energy consumption.

Whether small towns choose to adopt some of the strategies suggested here or develop their own, small towns of America have the potential to dispel the myth that the energy problem is beyond control and can be handled only by remote men of great power and expertise. The small town can make a real contribution toward successfully dealing with the energy crisis in the United States because of its scale, community spirit, and unity of image, and the results will be comparatively easy to measure in terms of energy savings and life quality gains.

NOTES

¹In *Small Town*, 7 (Nov. 1976), 7–13. For background on many of the suggestions furnished, see particularly pp. 8–9, 10–13.

²Ruth S. Foster, *Landscaping that Saves Energy Dollars* (New York: David McKay, 1978), pp. 50–51.

³Edward Mazria, *The Passive Solar Energy Book* (Emmous, Pa.: Rodale Press, 1979), pp. 90–91.

⁴Marshall Hunt and David Bainbridge, "The Davis Experience," *Solar Age*, 3 (May 1978), 22.

⁵James F. Barker, Eugene L. Bodycott and Richard Maxwell, "Movement as Related to the Success or Failure of an Urban Area: A Study of the Central West End of St. Louis," Thesis, Washington Univ., 1973, p. 71.

⁶Barker, p. 71.

Vision to Reality:
How to Achieve Architectural Quality in Small Towns

ROBERT M. FORD

The title of this paper suggests two propositions: that there is some value or benefit to achieving architectural quality; and that, if a need to achieve quality exists, we do not now have it in sufficient measure. Let us briefly examine both propositions.

We might begin by examining whether architecture is important to us as individuals and as a society. Nathanial Owings once called architecture the printing press of all ages, saying that it leaves in its structures a description of the society in which it works.[1] Through their architecture past generations have told us much about our past—about the dominating political forces, the values placed on certain institutions, the evolution of the culture as affected by industrialization, urbanization and corporate power and the frustrated desire for individuality in a mass production society. Architecture includes all aspects of our man made environment. Even the freeway speaks eloquently of the values, and perhaps the mistakes, of our time. If architecture reflects our values and if, as some social scientists maintain, we are products of culture and our environment, then we clearly have an important stake in acheiving a better designed environment and better architecture.

In looking at the second proposition suggested by the title, we must ask whether we presently lack architectural quality. As we consider the propositions raised here, it will be instructive to focus on some specific examples of small towns, and for this purpose I should like to turn to the South, particularly to the towns of Mississippi.

If we were asked to list the buildings or places of architectural quality in our community, the list would probably be very short. If we removed from our list those buildings built before 1940, we would likely find few if any buildings remaining. In most Mississippi towns the best architecture is represented by the antebellum homes of a few wealthy families and, if the town is old enough, occasionally by some significant churches. Some Mississippi towns boast handsome, unpretentious commercial structures surrounding park-like squares or a courthouse of quality and significance. These town squares, the legacy of a more leisurely life style, are related to pedestrians rather than automobiles. They represent a pace of life, a dignity and taste not prevalent in today's ubiquitous commercial strip with its profusion of McDonald's, Wendy's, Kentucky Fried Chicken and Captain Quik stores.

If most of our quality architecture has been passed on to us from another era, we need to understand how this achievement in the past was realized. It seems incongruous that in a time of increased technological capability, an enlightened and educated citizenry, and reasonable social and economic well being, we seem less able to achieve quality than were our forebears.

If we examine the past we find that few Mississippi towns had their own architects, although designers were occasionally brought in from the East. Indeed, architectural education in this country is a relatively recent development. Traditionally, architecture was promulgated through exposure to European examples or to variations of traditional styles described in books on architectural theory written by architects or other "gentlemen of taste." These books, along with a number of simpler pattern-books, served as guides for the numerous craftsmen-builders active throughout our area. Originality was not emphasized; it was more common and acceptable to select a design of proven taste and modify it to the environment and to particular requirements.

The influence of the Southern environment helped generate the "dog-trot" house. Raised on piers to avoid moisture, split into two segments divided by a central breezeway, utilizing cross ventilation in every room, and provided with wide sheltering roofs to give protection from the intense sun and heavy rains, the dog-trot represented a unique folk architecture of high quality.

In public buildings such as courthouses and churches, there was much emphasis placed on quality. Seemingly, the public's business occupied a higher place in the earlier society's scale of values than it presently does. Further, there seemed to be a consensus that if something were worth doing, it was worth doing well. We do not often find comparable quality in today's building.

One of the reasons is of course economic. Material, labor, land, and financing costs are significantly higher than in past eras. Yet if we examine benefits—particularly in public buildings—we see that the per capita cost difference between poor and excellent quality is relatively insignificant. In fact, good design may reduce costs.

Another reason that it is frequently difficult to achieve good architecture is that today's client is often poorly equipped to evaluate architectural quality. The client, whether businessman, doctor, school board member, or politician, is often less sensitive to good design then were his elitist predecessors who relied on accepted styles or pattern books. The client who knows a great deal about running his farm or business or political office should not necessarily be expected to show expertise in esthetics and design.

A third reason underlying the lack of quality in Mississippi architecture—indeed United States architecture—can be attributed to a society that fails to demand the level of quality in its built environment that it has come to expect in health care, technical support systems, automobiles, and clothes. But appreciation for good environment is growing, and more and more people are discovering the qualities from a previous architectural age once taken for granted. Appreciation for fine contemporary design is also growing, but at a painfully slow rate. This emerging appreciation for architectural and environmental quality needs encouragement. Projects, particularly public buildings, must be designed to the highest possible standards in order to demonstrate the quality of design which should be commonplace.

As my subtitle suggests, however, I do not intend simply to bemoan the existing situation, but rather to articulate ways in which architectural quality might be achieved. Let me make four specific suggestions.

(1) As responsible decision makers and participants in the modification of our environment, we must insist that excellent design be a fundamental goal. We must keep in mind that if one intends to do something, he or she must be willing to commit that little extra effort required to do it well.

(2) We should support architects in our communities who exhibit the desire and ability to provide quality architecture. The Mississippi chapter of the American Institute of Architects, through its Honor Awards Program, recognizes architects who have shown excellence in design. Work of these architects should be exhibited in every community to help build awareness of the potential which exists for good design.

(3) We should not be afraid to go outside our state or region to secure excellence in design. Our ancestors had the good judgment to do so on occasion and we still reap the rewards of their actions. One excellent contemporary example of this process can be found in the small town of Columbus, Indiana, which has sought out the best architectural

talent in the nation and in the process has become a unique repository of contemporary architectural quality.[2]

Like many small Mississippi towns Columbus, Indiana, has a number of affluent citizens who have lived and prospered in the community over many generations, people who have a special pride and sense of responsibility. In Columbus, J. Irwin Miller, representing the seventh generation of a local family who had founded the Cummins diesel company and established the local bank, recognized that really excellent architectural services would cost little more than ordinary levels of service. He determined therefore to bring in nationally renowned architects to design several buildings over which he had some influence. These buildings included churches, a number of banks and industrial facilities. Recognizing the unusually high caliber of architectural design that was achieved, Miller expanded his patronage to include public buildings. He paid all of the architectural fees for the buildings for which he was given the right to select the architects.

These projects, and others not supported directly by Miller but designed by respected architects throughout the United States, have gained international acclaim for Columbus as a unique center of excellent architectural design. Buildings developed under this program have included schools, a post office, restoration of store fronts on the Main Street and a new downtown shopping mall.

While there may not be an Irwin Miller in every town, there are a number of people in small towns who could begin to duplicate the achievement of Columbus, Indiana. These people should be sought out and encouraged to leave a legacy in the form of a quality environment that would give pleasure and a positive model for many years to come.

(4) In order to help make the vision of architectural quality become reality, consideration should be given to selecting architects through open design competitions. While this idea is not common, and in fact will be looked upon with disfavor by some of my colleagues in the architectural profession, I believe it to be one of the most efficient ways to achieve architectural quality in small towns.

Let me describe an architectural competition, give examples of the quality of work which can be achieved through this method of select-

Cultural Center, Biloxi, Mississippi. Architect: William Turnbull (Photo: Robert Ford)

ing an architect, discuss procedures and the very nominal extra cost of this method of selection, and then describe two recent competitions in Mississippi.

A competition is held to select an architect who offers the best insight and ability to design a particular building. It is not a method of reducing fees, but rather of finding the best possible design solution while working within the normally accepted fee structure associated with a particular building type.

A proper architectural design competition is run according to a strict and detailed set of rules—a competition code—the purpose of which is to assure fairness, prevent abuse of competitors, and guide the sponsor in establishing procedures. Essential to a competition code are a professional advisor to manage the competition for the sponsor, a clear building program, a qualified jury to select the winner, a strict time schedule, and adequate awards for the winners.

Evidence of the benefit of competitions is clear. Typically, those countries whose overall architectural quality is very high utilize open architectural design competitions as a commonplace architect selection method. Switzerland, Germany, all the Scandinavian countries, and, to a large extent, France, Italy, and Israel all employ this technique. They utilize open competitions not just for the occasional architectural monument, but for everyday buildings—a bus shelter, school, or library. They also use them for housing, town planning, and landscape design.

If competitions are so prevalent in Europe, one might ask, why have they not been used here in the United States? They have been, in fact, though on a modest scale. But even the few examples to date affirm the benefits of open design competitions. Some major results of design competitions are Central Park in New York, and the national capitol in Washington. More recent competitions have resulted in a number of new academic and state government buildings: the Jefferson Arch in St. Louis and the internationally acclaimed Boston City Hall. It is interesting that of the thirty finalists in the recent competition for the new Pompidou Cultural Center in Paris, ten were Americans and the winners were American trained.

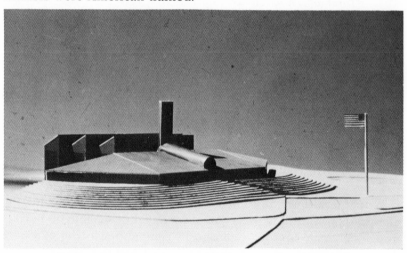

Fire Station Competition. Third Place. Architects: Henry P. Hildebrandt and Gary A. Shafer (Photo: Hildebrandt and Shafer)

*Fire Station Competition. Second Place. Architects: James
F. Barker and Dennis Ruth (Photo: James Barker)*

Now let me examine two examples closer to home: the first on the
Gulf coast in Biloxi, and the second in Starkville, Mississippi. In 1974
the city of Biloxi decided to build a new library and cultural center in
conjunction with renewal of its central business district. William
McMinn, of Mississippi State University's School of Architecture, was
asked to involve students in generating alternatives for the new center. Dean McMinn recognized that an excellent opportunity existed to
benefit both the academic needs of the new School of Architecture
and the citizens of Biloxi. He proposed that Biloxi invite six nationally
known architects to come to Biloxi, each spending a very intensive
week formulating a design proposal for the new facility. Further, the
School of Architecture, along with other Southern architectural
schools, would send students to assist each of the design teams,
building models and delineating drawings. The students would
benefit from their apprenticeship role with these outstanding architects, and Biloxi would benefit by having six excellent design
proposals. The very intensive week, with each team spending up-
wards of 500 man-hours, ended with the presentation of models and
drawings to a town meeting of 400 interested citizens. Subsequently,
William Turnbull of San Francisco was selected by the mayor to
develop his proposal into a schematic design and ultimately to pre-

pare architectural documents, call for bids, and supervise construction.

The building resulting from this process, which is actually a variation of the competition, is now complete and represents a very special place responding to unique needs of Biloxi. The quality of design is signified by the extensive coverage the project has received in national architectural publications.[3]

An example of a typical competition is represented by a fire station recently completed in Starkville, which is the home of Mississippi State University.[4] The town's board of aldermen was attempting to create a high quality fire station within a very limited budget. Because of a desire for accountability, the competition was limited to licensed architects in the immediate three county area. The program called for a 5,000 square foot building to house three fire engines with living and sleeping accommodations for fifteen men. The site on a corner lot required a clear and efficient functional organization and drive through bays so that trucks would not have to be backed into their stalls.

In all, eight designs were submitted, each including scaled drawings and a model. Projects were evaluated and prizes awarded by an outside jury of experts. The third place entry, submitted by Gary Shafer and Hank Hildebrandt, represented a strong image and an efficient, energy conscious design. Living quarters were set into earth berms for thermal protection. The three truck bays were articulated to express the vehicles housed inside. A symbolic hose drying tower atop a bright red metallic building gave clear statement that this was a fire station. This project was awarded a prize of $400.

The second place $600 award went to James Barker and Dennis Ruth, who designed a unique though functional fire station, also with a strong image. Major emphasis was placed on internal relationships, with trucks immediately accessible from sleeping facilities on one side and living spaces on the other. A "contextural wall" buffered the south sun and enframed an old fire engine which had served the Starkville community for many years. Curved walls suggested the dynamic movement inherent in firefighting.

As with other solutions, the winning design, submitted by Robert

Fire Station Competition. First Place. Architect: Robert M. Ford (Photo: Robert Ford)

M. Ford, featured efficient circulation of trucks and firemen. A traditional fire pole allowed direct access from second floor sleeping quarters to the truck area. Major features included a 40 foot glass showwindow, behind which the ladder truck was to be parked on display, and a series of southern oriented skylights intended to provide winter heat to the vehicle area. Image and symbol were extremely important. The disciplined and dangerous nature of firefighting was reflected in the highly regimented yet dynamic quality of the building.

Fire-engine-red interior paint used on ceilings and as accent was meant to contrast dramatically with more neutral concrete block walls and the galvanized metal roof. Instead of a cash prize, the award was a contract for the normal architectural commission. Thus the cost for this competition to the city of Starkville was only the $1,000 allocated as second and third prizes plus transportation and honoraria for jury members.

At this point it should be noted that the purpose of a design competition is not to achieve a final design but rather to select a direction, or what architects call a "schematic design." According to architect Charles Moore,[5] a competition jury is responsible for picking an architect with the competence and the approach to work with the client to achieve a final design, to make construction documents, and to get the building built. Once the architect has been selected through the competition process, he has the same responsibilities any other architect would have to make the building conform to the client's demands. Thus the competition design is really just the first step in a more involved process.

Although a firm budget ceiling for the Starkville fire station had not been established at the time of submission, the original competition design was fully developed and complete architectural drawings and specifications prepared. The project was bid and construction contracts tentatively drawn, based on a low bid of $196,000. At this point the mayor and a majority of the aldermen decided they could not afford to spend in excess of $150,000 for a fire station. This significant budget restriction, coming so late, necessitated redefinition of the program, reduction in building area, and changes in visual expression. A revised design was developed which the contractor then agreed to build for $146,000.

The revised plan is still quite similar to the orginal competition entry. The original skylight system, which would have resulted in energy savings over the life of the building, did have to be replaced by a less expensive flat roof. In order to provide the design with an image appropriate to a fire station, the large glass windows for exhibiting the fire engine were retained. The building was sheathed in light gauge metal to reflect the machine-like qualities of the vehicles housed within. Functional and image expressive elements such as a fire pole and rotating red alarm lights were maintained. The resulting building has generated praise from firemen, local citizens and visiting architects.

I should like to conclude with four brief thoughts about what kinds of visions lead to the reality of better designed environments and improved architectural quality: (1) we need to develop pride in every-

*Fire Station, Starkville, Mississippi. As Built. Architect:
Robert M. Ford (Photo: Robert Ford)*

thing we do and build; (2) we should be realistic about budgets and
resolve our priorities; (3) we need to consider carefully what our
direction should be; and (4) we should seek out people with the vision
and capabilities necessary to insure a satisfying living environment—one which reinforces sense of place, employs appropriate
symbol and image, and which reflects the most worthwhile goals of
our time.

NOTES

[1]"Nathaniel Owings, *The American Aesthetic* (New York: Harper and Row, 1969),
p. 153.

[2]See Barclay Gordon, "Industrial Buildings: Toward Higher Standards for Design,"
Architectural Record, 151 (May 1972), 114–17; John Morris Dixon, "Piazza, American
Style," *Progressive Architecture*, 57 (June 1976), 64–69; and William Marlin, "Medici
of the Midwest," *Architectural Forum*, 140 (March 1974), 47–57.

[3]For a description of the competition process and photographs documenting the
resulting building, see Gerald Allen, "Biloxi Library and Cultural Center," *Architectural Record*, 163 (May 1978), 103–08; and "The First Biloxi Design Festival," *Architectural Record*, 157 (May 1975), 107–10.

[4]See Paul Roberson, "Two Mississippi Design Competitions," *Mississippi Ar-*

chitect, 9 (1978), 4; and Robert M. Ford, "A Fire Station for Starkville," *Mississippi Architect*, 9 (1978), 5. First, second, and third place entries were submitted by members of the faculty of the Mississippi State University School of Architecture.

[5]Charles A. Moore, *The Yale Mathematics Building Competition: Architecture For a Time of Questioning* (New Haven: Yale Univ. Press, 1974), p. viii.

Tradition and Continuity in Architecture:
Toward a More Rational and Democratic Environmental Process

RONALD MURRAY

The inability to construct the contemporary urban environment with any real aesthetic amenity has surely been one of the most inauspicious lapses of modern society. Unfortunately, even the small town or village faced with the opportunity for growth has been as likely as cities to suffer from aesthetically unrelated and chaotic new building, as well as from an unnecessary destruction of the existing fabric. While such trends are largely attributable to economic and political forces beyond the control of the architect, modern theories of design have also helped perpetuate and legitimize the lack of coherence and continuity that characterizes the environmental norm. Indeed, modernism has propagated an architecture almost completely void of contextural response, an architecture that has contributed to an environment of isolated buildings, most of which exhibit little sense of historical continuity or local character, and a large number of which go unappreciated by the public.

The early modernists, in dogmatic and revolutionary terms, consciously rejected past styles and vocabularies, believing that their work was "the expression of some unchallengeable 'need' or requirement inherent in the twentieth century with which we must conform."[1] The resulting wholesale rejection of tradition has crippled the language of architecture by divesting it of all familiar structures, symbols and images and by sacrificing much of the beauty, richness, depth and meaning of the accumulated talent of its history. In fact, the loss of a publicly accepted language in architecture, as well as the accelerating loss of tradition and convention in modern society, threatens to destroy the basis of cultural cohesion and communication, of rational and democratic growth and change.

The roots of such a denial lie deep in Western history, as suggested by William McClung in a recent manuscript, *The Architecture of Paradise,* and as alluded to by Colin Rowe in his recent book, *Collage City;* they may even be traced to Western man's religious estrangement from God and Nature. From biblical writing to Plato, from Seneca to Laugier, Violet-le-Duc, Corbusier and Wright, we see evidence of the quest for a spiritual reunification of Man and Nature or God. We see on the one hand a search for a pure, primitive Edenic past, before the "degeneracy" of culture and convention, and on the other, for a redemptive utopian future, beyond the irrationalities and evils of cultural man. In either case, culture and its conventional expressions have been seen as the realm of "fallen man." It has been through the association with a Nature outside of culture, expressed in either idealized utopian visions or in a natural Arcadian past, that man throughout history has attempted to legitimize his craft, particularly his architecture.[2] George Santayana has written that "man has a prejudice against himself; anything which is a product of his mind seems to him to be unreal or comparatively insignificant. We are satisfied only when we fancy ourselves surrounded by objects and laws independent of our own nature."[3]

In distrust of cultural direction, then, the development of architecture in the modern era has in large part been an attempt to define the universal imperatives. In twentieth century America Frank Lloyd Wright attempted to legitimize his "organic" architecture through a visual and spiritual conformity with nature; in Europe an architecture developed that was no less intent on moral legitimization through conformity with nature, only there nature was defined as the universal laws of mathematics, primal geometries, and indirectly of the machine and technology.[4] Both definitions were thus acultural; in fact, in the words of Johannes Itten, the influential instructor of design at the Bauhaus, one of the earliest schools of modernism, ". . . every student arrives encumbered with a mass of accumulated information which must be abandoned . . . [in order to] acquaint him with the basic principles which underly all creative activity in the visual arts."[5] Reyner Banham points out that Itten thereby encouraged ". . . the liberation of innate sensibilities, not the acquirement of knowledge; . . . the destruction of previous training, not its exploitation . . ."[6]

Thus modernism in architecture not only envisioned a literal social utopia based on the universal laws of nature, it believed that these universal laws could be intuited by the creative imagination quite aside from traditional objective reason. It made the assumption that the new technological world, by freeing us from our cultural past, would provide the basis for the attainment of a just and egalitarian society. It sought to use architecture as a symbol of the new vision, an architecture unencumbered by images of class hierarchy or social status, an architecture pure in shape and spirit, innocently functional and beyond the pretension of style.

Idealistic and obviously impelling in a troubled world, this new vision and, finally, the new architecture, were destined to failure and reversal. The clean lines and pure geometric shapes, orginally intended to symbolize a liberation from the past, have almost universally come to symbolize the influence and power of modern corporate structure and the new ruling class. Thus the architecture that so heroically sought to reject such symbols of power, wealth and pretension, has in the end become one of their most visible means of expression. And interestingly, it has been modern architecture's antihistorical and anti-cultural (and therefore inherently anti-democratic) base that has allowed its utopian idealism to be absorbed and neutralized by a consumption-oriented economy which has had a tendency to deny cultural reference. In fact, such an economy thrives on deliberate and continual cultural revolution; in order to stimulate ever higher levels of consumption, in the words of Gerald Graff, "it has a built-in need to destroy all vestiges of tradition, all orthodox ideologies, and all continuous and stable forms of reality. The real avant-grade is advanced capitalism"[7] And regardless of its frequent anti-establishment rhetoric, architecture continues to offer itself as a willing accomplice. Bruno Zevi reiterated the modernist ideology as late as 1978, writing of the need to reject "a priori assumptions, set phrases, and conventions of every type and kind. The inventory springs from an act of cultural annihilation—what Roland Barthes called 'the zero degree of writing'—and leads to a rejection of all traditional norms and canons."[8]

The effect on contemporary society of this cultural negation, whether motivated by economics or ideology, has been devastating.

According to Christopher Lasch, one of America's foremost social historians, perhaps the most significant social characteristic of the modern era has been an indifference to and hostility toward the past, an indication, he believes, of a deep and serious cultural bankruptcy.[9] Such a denial of the past on the surface seems heroic, progressive and optimistic, but he asserts that it embodies the despair of a society unable to face its own future.[10] The past no longer holds out guidance to our actions; in our wholesale rejection of it we have lost the ability or the will to rationally and objectively evaluate it, and to separate that which is still valid and sustaining about it from that which is outmoded and over-restrictive. Indeed, we have come to hold such a narrowly instrumental view of knowledge that we assume it to be constantly rendered obsolete by rapid technological change. As a consequence, our faith in the generational transferability of knowledge and wisdom has suffered, the result being in part manifest in our worship of the "vigor of youth" and our disdain for experience and for the aged in our society.[11] Further, according to Lasch the result is more and more a general conversion of popular traditions of self-reliance, traditions normally passed from generation to generation, into esoteric knowledge administered by highly trained "experts," encouraging the belief that ordinary competence in any field is beyond the reach of the layman.[12] Earlier traditions of local action have been almost completely undermined by a modern bureaucratic industrial system that has come very near destroying craftsmanship, the work ethic, family life, and in fact all those institutions capable of sustaining the strength and confidence of the individual. The new paternalism that has emerged encourages the dependence of the individual more than ever on the state, the industrial system and on a professional and managerial elite.

The effective loss of cultural traditions on such a scale is surely one of the most threatening and frightening characteristics of our time; according to Lasch, it "makes talk of a New Dark Age" seem "far from frivolous."[13] Indeed, he implies that the very hope for Western society and its democratic traditions depends upon a respect for the past and the belief that in some ways the past might have been better, attitudes which neither derive from sentimental illusion nor lead to a "backward-looking" paralysis of will.[14] Quite the opposite: there is a firm philosophical basis for the belief that tradition and the past provide the foundations for all human efforts at rational thought. If we think about it, only in a situation where we can be reasonably sure of the consequences of our actions can there be any hope of acting rationally. A stranger in a foreign land totally unaware of the customs or language has little rational basis on which to pattern his attempts at communication.

Karl Popper, scientist and philosopher, asserts that human rationality and the development of science and knowledge depend on the past and our inherited traditions.[15] In fact, to assume that any universal or absolute truth is somehow manifest outside that cultural search, as the modernists did, is to hold a notion of truth as being within the potential authority of man, an idea that carries with it the most authoritarian of political implications. To remove oneself or one's ideas from a cultural frame of reference is to remove oneself from the possibility of critical examination. An open society must be based on the notion that all our sources of knowledge are subject to review and discussion.[16] Even the theories and hypotheses of science, Popper writes, are not necessarily universal truths, but represent a kind of theoretical framework, a shared frame of reference, traditions of a sort, open to critical examination and potential advancement. "The most important sources of knowledge are in fact tradition . . . the advances of knowledge consist mainly in the modification of earlier knowledge."[17] The critical and progressive, though not absolutist, character constitutes the rationality and objectivity of science. By trial and error modification, science has developed a certain capability to predict events in the physical world; without the cultural and historical frame of reference, of course, most of the acquired predictive ability would be lost, and further, there would be no basis for making new conjectures about the world.

In the social world language and tradition serve much the same purpose: they represent our shared frame of reference, and like science, while containing no claims to absolutism, they are the record of the continuing human search for some objective truth. They are the media of generational continuity, and in the words of Morton Bloomfield, "language is the basis of whatever social cohesion we can attain; to a large extent it defines our very humanity."[18] Language and tradition alike incorporate and preserve countless myths, theories, beliefs and wisdoms, extending throughout and to the depths of the culture.[19] Such a shared frame of reference allows us the predictive ability necessary for communication in the social world. Obviously a complete rejection of that traditional reference could lead only to a loss of shared images and perceptions and a resulting lack of communicability.

Because a free and open society so hinges on a shared and open communication, we then cannot escape tradition. But there are alternative ways of dealing with the past: one, of course, is an uncritical acceptance, often characterized by intolerance and dogma, though sometimes we are simply unaware of the traditions under which we operate. The other way to deal with tradition is through a critical attitude, depending neither on blind acceptance nor blind rejection, but based on an ongoing attempt to evaluate in an objective and open way.[20] In fact, it is only against this backdrop of a continuing critical appraisal of history and cultural traditions that we attain any critical perspective with which to judge our contemporary world. Isolated by an intolerance of tradition, objectivity is lost and we become enslaved by an unquestioning acceptance of our modern world. Concerning the prevalence of this predicament in modern society, Gerald Graff has written, "Contemporary culture contains few ideas capable of liberating us from its provincialism. On the contrary, it exudes warnings expressed in the most intimidating of styles, of the absolute futility of attempting to understand it and, even more, the absolute futility of trying to resist its charm."[21]

And so architecture, by its rejection of its tradition has suffered many of the same ills as the society at large. By being cut off from its cultural language and its tradition and history, it has witnessed a dramatic loss of communicability and has found itself unable to solve many of its basic problems of climatic response, comfort, beauty, transition and continuity. Sensing this, the profession has in the last decade or so frantically tried to interject "substance"—"scientific" problem-solving methodologies, "scientific" information from the social sciences, and so on, much of which has provided useful information but none of which has substituted for the cultural and human insights that are a part of the architectural tradition. As in the larger society, one result has been more and more dependence on "experts," a trend that has led to very little real and meaningful substance or truth. Another result has been the reliance more and more on the fads and fashions of the latest celebrity architect, seductively rendered by the beautiful and enticing photography of the modern media.

The continuing result is that modernism's narrow and closed language has allowed only a few of the "initiated" even to be considered seriously in their criticism. Certainly the public has little understood much of the resulting architecture; in fact, it is often shocked or offended by what it sees. Nevertheless most people assume that they are not authorities to judge and have slowly given in to "progress" and "modernity." Thus the rejection of a common language has not only weakened the depth and substance of architecture; it has also undermined the willingness and ability of the public and architects to criticize it and thereby exercise any real control over its future. We accept such architecture as the inevitable "expression of the age," self-justifying, not realizing the philosophical and even authoritarian consequences of such an acceptance.

Surely, a major task of the architectural profession must be to uphold, clarify and enrich our socially shared language and to maintain the critical appraisal of our traditions. Only then can we expect to educate a wider public to higher levels of appreciation, and perhaps more importantly, only then can we expect to allow the responsive feedback necessary for the trial and error improvement of our art and craft. And it must be understood that it is not we, as architects or even as human beings of a particular generation, who "invent" a language; language is a tradition and to a large degree a cultural given. Acceptance of that language should be no more limiting to the architect than to the poet; it offers an infinite richness upon which to draw. Furthermore, language is never static and unchangeable, nor is it absolutely precise and uninterpretable. All definitions, after all, depend on other definitions. While providing the framework for cultural cohesion, language at the same time offers the very instrument with which to describe, explain and argue about its inherent myths, beliefs and wisdoms.[22] It thus serves as the instrument not only for cultural cohesion but also for cultural growth and change. There is no reason that we cannot learn from our past and at the same time respond to our present and imagine for our future. As Colin Rowe has written:

> We must recognize the complementary relationship that is fundamental to the processes of anticipation and retrospection. They are inter-dependent activities; we cannot perform without exercising them both; no attempt to suppress either in the interest of the other can ever be protractedly successful. We may receive strength from the novelty of the prophetic declamation; but the degree of this potency must be strictly related to the known, perhaps even mundane and necessarily memory-laden context from which it emerged.[23]

Such an awareness of the continuity and inter-dependence of our past and of our future is indeed necessary to the rational and democratic development of our society, and of our architecture and environment.

NOTES

[1]David Watkin, *Morality and Architecture: The Development of a Theme in Architectural History and Theory from the Gothic Revival to the Modern Movement* (Oxford: Oxford Univ. Press, 1977), p. 9.

[2]William McClung, *The Country House in English Renaissance Poetry* (Berkeley: Univ. of California, 1977), pp. 12–13.

[3]Colin Rowe, *Collage City* (Cambridge, Mass.: M.I.T. Press, 1979), p. 2.

[4]William McClung, *The Architecture of Paradise* (Unpublished manuscript, 1979), Chap. 3.

[5]Reyner Banham, *Theory and Design in the First Machine Age* (New York: Praeger, 1960), p. 279.

[6]Banham, p. 279.

[7]Gerald Graff, *Literature Against Itself: Literary Ideas in Modern Society* (Chicago: Univ. of Chicago Press, 1979), p. 8.

[8]Bruno Zevi, *The Modern Language of Architecture* (Seattle: Univ. of Washington Press, 1978), p. 7.

[9]Christopher Lasch, *The Culture of Narcissism: American Life in an Age of Diminishing Expectations* (New York: W. W. Norton, 1978), p. xvii.

[10]Lasch, p. xviii.

[11]Lasch, p. 213.

[12]Lasch, p. 128.

[13]Lasch, p. 151.

[14]Lasch, p. xvii.

[15]Karl Popper, *Conjectures and Refutations: The Growth of Scientific Knowledge* (New York: Basic Books, 1963), p. 127.

[16]Popper, p. 27.
[17]Popper, p. 27.
[18]Morton Bloomfield, Introd., in *Language as a Human Problem*, ed. Morton Bloomfield and Einar Haugen (New York: W. W. Norton, 1973), p. xi.
[19]Popper, p. 130; see also Peter Berger and Thomas Luckman, *The Social Construction of Reality* (New York: Doubleday, 1967), p. 69.
[20]Popper, p. 120.
[21]Graff, p. 123.
[22]Popper, p. 135.
[23]Rowe, p. 49.

Types of American Small Towns and How to Read Them

FRED E. H. SCHROEDER

The first point I wish to make is so obvious that it may be wondered why anyone should bother to write it down; my second, so intuitively theoretical that it appears to be totally academic, in the worst sense of the word. The first thesis is simply stated: *small towns are not all alike*, but the second thesis deserves to be stated in academic jargon: *small towns possess architectonic signals that epitomize their covenants*. The appropriate responses are *so what?* and *who cares?*

In answering these common sense rejoinders, it is necessary to identify the primary audience that I am addressing. It is not architects, city planners, geographers or sociologists, though I think that they will benefit from tuning in, but rather some people whose very real concerns have never been addressed in understandable terms—those who are moving to a small town and who are in for some form of unexpected values adjustment, culture shock, disillusionment or even emotional breakdown unless they can be prepared with some practical, realistic and sympathetic means for "reading" the small town. (Although my definition of a "small town" could extend up to 25,000 population, I find that for the methods set forth here, 15,000 works best.)

Census studies of this decade indicate that not only are we speaking of a significant number of people, but that the number has been increasing.[1] Further, we know something about these people: they are well educated in the main, being professionals, government workers and employees of larger corporations, and their lifestyles are shaped more by mass society than by local traditions.[2] There are important differences in their values and goals from those of long time residents, however, and these must be acknowledged if the newcom-

104

ers are to make the best assessment of a small community as a place to live.

Their ideas of small towns derive from a variety of sources, including such fiction as Sinclair Lewis's *Main Street,* Mark Twain's "The Man who Corrupted Hadleyburg," Sherwood Anderson's *Winesburg, Ohio,* Erskine Caldwell's *God's Little Acre* and the works of William Faulkner, from such popular novels as Grace Metalious's *Peyton Place,* from films such as Norman Lear's 1971 *Cold Turkey,* Norman Jewison's 1967 *In the Heat of the Night,* and Stanley Kramer's 1952 *High Noon,* from television serials like *Gunsmoke, The Andy Griffith Show, Green Acres, The Little House on the Prairie, Palmerstown, U.S.A., The Waltons, Mannix* and *The Rockford Files,* and from Charles Kuralt's feature stories.[3] To a considerably lesser extent, people learn about small towns from the social sciences, especially geography and sociology. Unlike the media, which generalize by stereotype, the social sciences generalize by statistical tables, but either way the act of generalization erases differences among towns, both subtle and gross, and reinforces the view that small towns are all alike. It is remarkable to see the degree to which small town residents are themselves captured by the stereotypes. As Joseph P. Lyford concluded in one of the few good detailed studies of an individual town, *The Talk in Vandalia,* they are subject to "an unconscious absorption of many of the standard myths about small-town complacency, neighborliness, Godliness, stupidity, provincialism, loyalties, unity, freshness."[4]

My own experience underscores this. About ten years ago as a journeyman humanist for the National Humanities Series I spent more than a year traveling to several dozen towns throughout the United States, during which I developed a number of intuitive techniques for "reading" small towns, techniques that I have worked to articulate over the past seven years in a course called Rural Life Styles, designed for the second-year medical students in the Family Practice Program of the School of Medicine of the University of Minnesota, Duluth. Both explicitly and implicitly, the denizens of the towns I visited and many of the medical students (most of whom come from rural homes) expressed the idea that the stereotype produces not only a self-effacing apologetic tone, but debilitating feelings of inadequacy; for the students, the stereotype produces simplistic prejudgment that is as inappropriate to a newcomer to a strange community as it would be to a physician meeting a new patient. Thus the "so what" to my "obvious" thesis that small towns are *not* all alike is that the opposite view is not only common, but dangerous.

The most common stereotype of the small town is that of agricultural service center, an image that is not unreasonable since agriculture not only accounts for the historical origins of most towns and many cities in America, but probably continues to be the most common reality, especially for towns of a thousand population and less. The location of the bank, the implement dealership, the grocery, the auto service station, the post office and the lunch counter, it will also be the center for the consolidated school, several churches, and the processing-distribution plant for the area produce. But the last item introduces variety, for there is a world of difference between Odanah (150) with wild rice, Valders (900) with milk and eggs, Eagle River (1400) with cranberries, Viroqua (3800) with tobacco, and Sturgeon Bay (7200) with cherries (all five of these agricultural centers being in the state of Wisconsin.) Then consider Foley, Alabama (3400), with pecans; Pittsfield, Illinois (4300), hogs; Crisfield, Maryland (3100), shellfish; Buffalo, Wyoming (3400), beef cattle and sheep; Presque Isle, Maine (12,000), potatoes; LeSueur, Minnesota (3800), peas and sweet corn; and Tontitown, Arkansas (500), vineyards.[5]

But this is the most elementary geography, you might reply. Indeed it is, but recall the stereotype. In addition, a listing of different agricultural products, even where it implies different climates, natural flora, different seasonal cycles, and different life styles disguises other significant differences. For example, Odanah is tribal headquarters for the Bad River Chippewa; Eagle River, Sturgeon Bay and Buffalo are recreational resort centers; Foley manufactures furniture and clocks; Buffalo, Eagle River, Pittsfield, Sturgeon Bay and Viroqua are county seats. In pointing out that "agricultural service centers" are not alike, I should note that I have not mentioned wheat, rice, oranges, wool, timber, lettuce, sugar beets, cotton, catfish, maple syrup, horses, hops, ducks and tulips.

For other types of small towns I shall try to be less prolix with examples, but I will suggest some of the lifestyle differences that are implied. County seats, for instance, mean that attorneys will live there, that there will very likely be a newspaper, and that the town will not die. State capitals, such as Olympia, Washington (26,000), Frankfort, Kentucky (25,000), Helena, Montana (24,000), Dover, Delaware (23,000), Augusta, Maine (22,000), Juneau, Alaska (18,000), Pierre, South Dakota (11,000), Montpelier, Vermont (9000), multiply these characteristics, as well as bearing with them a degree of social and cultural elegance that sets them well apart from most larger cities. In addition, Annapolis, Bismarck, Concord, Jefferson City and Lincoln have populations under 35,000 while Santa Fe and Cheyenne are under 50,000. There are over 3000 counties in the United States, and, even after discounting larger county seats such as Chicago, Newark and Los Angeles, or Dayton, Davenport and Duluth, one is left with a considerable number of small towns that are unique because of being legal and judicial centers. Related to the government legislative centers are towns that are governmental social service centers, such as penitentiary and mental hospital towns. Many of these are also agricultural centers, as well as being especially "pretty" towns, such as Cherokee, Iowa (7300), Chillicothe, Ohio (23,000) and Waupun, Wisconsin (8000). These towns are exceptional in having to cope with an uncomplimentary regional image, for it is an American folkway to refer to the *institution* by the name of the *town*, so that all citizens are unfairly associated with mental illness or moral turpitude. These towns also will have an unusual concentration of professionals in medicine, psychology and social work.

The industrial small town is rarely part of the popular stereotype. At one extreme is the company town, such as Kohler, Wisconsin (1800), an idyllically built and landscaped project of the famous plumbing-fixture firm, Hershey, Pennsylvania (9000) of chocolate-bar fame, and the much younger Silver Bay, Minnesota (3500), built in 1956 by Reserve Mining Company to process and ship taconite ore. These towns are born in profit-seeking benevolence and energetic optimism, but the full realization of dependence, whether it comes from hard times in production, from union strife or from environmental conflicts, gives a peculiar psychological character to such communities. Paranoiac is the best label for those company towns that have gone through a crucible of lay-offs, bitter strikes, or the abandonment of mines, forests or industrial plants. But in the upswing, theirs is the Good Life: richly endowed public schools, recreation programs, libraries, neat cottages, fresh natural environment, and unity of purpose. The "model towns" like Kohler are rare enough, but those that have been adjuncts of mines and oil fields constitute a significant number.

The company town is the extreme kind of industrial small town, but its utter dependency upon a single economic source is a spectre to haunt many small towns. The common story of community efforts to keep or to replace the local industry, and to diversify, is well chronicled in *The Talk in Vandalia*, while the examples of declining small towns like Ironwood, Michigan (7700), and larger cities such as Gary, Indiana (originally a model company town), Elmira, New York, New Castle, Pennsylvania, and Highland Park, Michigan, serve as reminders that one-industry existence is precarious for all.[7] But in a town of 2000 the closing of one industry with one hundred employees could produce a 25 percent population reduction and leave dozens of empty homes. Such bleak outlooks should not be overemphasized, however, for healthy industrial towns are abundant. Some examples will indicate how some small town industries have attained major successes. Rogers, Arkansas (11,000), is the home of Daisy airguns; Pendleton, Oregon (14,000), of Pendleton Woolens; New Holstein, Wisconsin (3000), of Tecumseh engines; Hesston, Kansas (2000), of Hesston harvesting machinery. All these towns are economically viable because of active production or diversified activity (including agricultural service center), and some are themselves the corporate centers maintaining branch plants or offices in metropolitan cities. The effect on life styles is opposite of the stereotypes. Civic pride, boosterism, quality restaurants and motels, country clubs, airports and a continuous communication with sophisticated urban fashions in clothing, appetites, conversation and recreational activities take one equally far from Tobacco Road or Archie Bunker's corner bar in Brooklyn. An industrial town subtype that is rather less fortunate, but similar in social style, is the type whose industry is a branch of a major corporation or conglomerate. These are increasingly common, differing from company towns in the industry's not having created the town, or owning it. There is, however, an impersonal, ruthless pattern of abandonment among these faceless corporations whose homes are in New York City, Tokyo and Berlin, and whose remote source of real power may reside in Athens, Geneva or Saudi Arabia. The social psychological effects of the more or less dependence on remote powers are rather harshly described in Vidich and Bensman's 1958 classic *Small Town in Mass Society,* in which local naivete and self-delusion are, I think, overemphasized,[8] at least if they are taken as universally applicable or descriptive of 1980s America.

A related town type is the military reservation, where economic dependence is similar and abandonment is not quite so cavalier, but where direct social and political involvement in community affairs is limited. Hy Averback's uneven film, *Suppose They Gave a War and Nobody Came* (1970, retitled *War Games* for television), is at once an analysis, a parody and a stereotype of this type. A last subtype is the bedroom community, epitomized in New Canaan, Connecticut (18,000), where sumptuous houses for a time had an average tenure of ownership of three years, being stopping places for high executives in many Manhattan corporations, and Burnsville, Minnesota (20,000), whose mercurial growth was largely due to commuters to diverse offices of Minneapolis and St. Paul. These, as Richard Lamb demonstrates statistically (though with a notable lack of reference to any real town, city or human being) in his *Metropolitan Impacts on Rural America* (1975), are undergoing change but continue to be the predominant area of small town growth,[9] producing what Werner Z. Hirsch has named "the polynucleated metropolis."[10] Although these are usually parts of Standard Metropolitan Statistical Areas (SMSA), they *are* small towns in which the local shopping center, school, country club, church, bank and home have greater direct influence upon family life styles than do the metropolitan cultural institutions, downtowns, and corporate places of employment. Civic pride, progressive optimism, and a frenzy for cultural uplift rivalled only by the drive for material splendor are characteristics, along with drug problems in the schools and some sort of variant on the 1950s syndromes of *The Lonely Crowd* and *The Organization Man*. But as with all my generalizations, predictions of individual values and life styles should never be presumed.

One of the common stereotypes about small towns is that they are "slower-paced" or "sleepy," contrasting with the big city stereotypes of "fast-paced," "exciting," "stimulating" and so on. One type of small town that opposes this image is the tourist center. The prototype, I like to think, is Canterbury, England, where the party started in Chaucer's day and hasn't stopped yet. In the United States, Niagara Falls and Saratoga Springs, New York, Long Branch, New Jersey, and Hot Springs, Arkansas, are early examples that have undergone changes due to growth or decline. But others continue to thrive as small towns: Margaretville, New York (800), is a Catskills summer resort, a spring fishing center and a fall hunting center; Eureka Springs, Arkansas (1700), is an Ozark center; Wisconsin Dells (2400) is Chicago's playground; Grand Marais (1300) is one of Minnesota's outfitting ports for both wilderness canoeing and Lake Superior fishing; Red Lodge, Montana (1900), and Jackson, Wyoming (1300), are two of the West's many outfitting and dude ranch centers. Related to these are the "wide-open" rest and recuperation towns, some, like Covington, Kentucky, and Reno, Nevada, still wide-open, but overgrown for our definition of small towns; others, like Hurley, Wisconsin (2500), no longer so exclusively serving lumberjacks and miners, but hunters, fishermen and skiers instead, while trying to clean up the residual image of gambling, barroom brawls and red-light district; or Dodge City, Kansas (17,000), still serving ranch hands but exploiting its raunchy history for family tourists; still others, like Valdez, Alaska (1100), newly booming for construction "roughnecks" along with other pioneer types.

Whether we are speaking of the tourist town or the "R & R" town, activity, snarled traffic, crowds of pedestrians and a welter of sounds and smells not only differentiate these towns from many others, but from each other. The natural environment is one important factor, but the cycles of visiting are more important, whether seasonal or weekly, for the *off-season* bares the "real community," whose population statistics belie the seasonal crowding. The "real community" comes closer to the small town image than the seasonal visitors might suppose, although it is primarily service business (resorts, motels, restaurants, gift shops, food specialities, real estate, recreational hardware), which represents a quite different relationship to the natural surroundings than that in an agricultural or mining center. Also, many members of the business community are themselves seasonal citizens.

A subtype of the tourist town is the arts center, whose existence gives the lie to the popular conception of the cultural vacuum in small towns. Gatlinburg, Tennessee (2900), is a common type, where sophisticated potters, weavers, painters, interior designers and architects constitute a significant portion of the population that serves the tourist trade. Taos, New Mexico (2500), and Provincetown, Massachusetts (3000), have for many decades been the permanent or seasonal homes of major artists and writers, and almost all states have small towns that are not necessarily resort areas but contain a disproportionate number of professional artists and designers as well as knowledgeable patrons, collectors and dealers. Most of these towns possess architectural quaintness or a heavy aura of historical association, like Concord, Massachusetts (6500 town center), Galena, Illinois (4000), Mineral Point, Wisconsin (2400). Another type is the organized arts colony. Elbert Hubbard's East Aurora, New York (7100), may have been one of the oldest, but Chautauqua, New York, whose population fluctuates annually between 4300 and 10,000, continues to be the prototype as well as a namesake of all small town intellectual-artistic colonies, such as Aspen, Colorado (2500).

Many, many small towns are college or university centers: some, like Hanover, New Hampshire (6200), Northfield, Minnesota (11,000), or Princess Anne, Maryland (1000), where higher education is almost the sole industry; others, like Mathiston, Mississippi (600), Hesston, Kansas (2000), New Paltz, New York (6000), Grinnell, Iowa (8500) and Moscow, Idaho (16,000), where education combines to a varying degree with agriculture, manufacturing, government, or recreation. Students and faculty alike invest these towns with unusual personalities, marked not only by lectures and recitals, but by ethnic food restaurants, craft shops, bookstores, recreational equipment stores and an inordinate amount of bicycle and pedestrian traffic during the academic year.

To summarize here, big cities—and we have barely thirty of them with a population in excess of a half million—are usually regarded as unique and individual, while small towns are generalized and stereotyped. Yet more than one-fifth of the nation lives in more than 5500 cities with populations between 2500 and 25,000, while another 5 percent lives in over *thirteen thousand* places of less than 2500— "places," because the census bureau classifies these as rural non-farm rather than as towns and townspeople.[11] In short, the sheer number of small cities and towns is justification for generalization. But studious generalization, no matter how rational, and popular stereotype, no matter how veritable, erase individual differences, and such erasure confounds the individual's ability to judge small cities and towns as places to work and live. A partial remedy is to subdivide the general into smaller, though still broad, types based upon predominant economic function. Thus we have named seven major town types: the *agricultural center*, the *government center*, the *industrial town*, the *polynuclear suburb*, the *recreational town*, the *art colony* and the *college town*, with the understanding that there are numerous subtypes, an endless variety of mixtures and several other types not mentioned, such as Indian reservation towns, Interstate highway cloverleafs, crossroad hamlets, retirement villages, mobile-home parks, ports and terminuses of railroads and highways. Each of these implies different life styles, different social and occupational population concentrations and different arrays of community values. Identification of the broad town type to which an individual community belongs is relatively easy, but identification of the unique values is not. To introduce one technique of making such an identification, we should look at an eighth major town type, the *covenanted community*.

This term is borrowed directly from Page Smith's *As a City Upon a Hill: The Town in American History*.[12] As will be seen, I expand his definition for the purpose of "reading" a town, but his definition and thesis should be stated before I manipulate them. *Covenant*, of course, is a legal term meaning an agreement between parties. In

American history, *covenant* bears Biblical connotations along with its
legal meaning. The agreements between Jehovah and the chosen
people, represented by Adam, Noah, Abraham and Moses, were set
forth as *covenants* rather than autocratic *dictates*. Thus, in the historical and symbolic prototype of American towns, Plymouth, the term
covenant in the *Mayflower Compact* is the solemn keyword, as it is
ten years later for Massachusetts Bay Colony. From these first origins
the covenanted community develops, as Page Smith summarizes,
"composed of individuals bound in a special compact with God and
with each other. The ties extend vertically within the society, uniting
the classes and the society to God. . . . one of the most important
attributes of the covenanted community was that it could reproduce
itself almost to infinity once its essential form had become fixed. Each
community was simply a congregation produced by fission from the
old community. . . . It was only a common faith, a shared covenant, that
held the community together. . . ." Page Smith continues later, "Long
neglected by historians, who have been inclined to assume that American towns have had exclusively economic origins, the colonized
towns have been far more numerous and far more important than
historians have recognized" and he sets forth several major subtypes:[13] (1) colonized from a home town or county, for example, Worth-
ington, Ohio (16,000), formed by settlers from Granby, Connecticut
(6200); (2) colonized from scattered communities but subscribing to a
common faith or ideal, such as Quaker towns like Salem, Iowa (5100),
or Newport, Indiana (700); (3) the foreign or ethnic community such as
the Dutch Zeeland, Michigan (4800), or German St. Nazianz, Wisconsin (800); (4) the secular communal experiment, such as the Fourierist
Red Bank, New Jersey (13,000), the Noyes Oneida, New York community (12,000), the Pietist Amana, Iowa (600), or the temperance
Greeley, Colorado (39,000).

The examples given are historical: many such towns have disappeared, others have totally lost their original character, while others,
like the Oneida and the Amana communities continue in altered forms
with national reputations for industry (Oneida silver, Amana re-
frigerators, microwave ovens, woolens). But this sort of primary covenanted colony is far from dead, as can be seen in The Farm community

of Summertown, Tennessee (1200), which began in San Francisco's Haight-Ashbury "greening" of the late 1960s. The first farm, organized in 1971, was followed by seventeen more "Farm" colonies. The Farm's covenant is in the best American tradition and bears quotation from a recent brochure:

> We are more than just a community, for we are committed to each other and to a spiritual agreement. We've shared a vision of a world full of love, and we know that Spirit is real. The way we know we can make a difference is to get strong and take care of the business at hand: to feed the hungry, to shelter the homeless, to heal the sick, and to share what we've learned. This all requires commitment.
>
> Some of our agreements are pretty basic. We agree about being complete vegetarians, about being nonviolent, about telling the truth. We agree about being collective and sharing fortunes. It says in the *Bible,* "And all who believed were together and had all things in common; and they sold their possessions and goods and distributed them to all, as any had need" (Acts 2:44-45). We hold our land in common and no money is exchanged for any goods or services within the community.
>
> We are not just a religion. We are a living spiritual village/church. Teachings emerge continuously in our being together.[14]

Thus, the covenanted community is the last major town type. The communal experiment, whether old, like the Amanas, or new, like The Farms, is one living form, but a mixture of ethnic and religious factors gives uniquely consistent character to the spiritual and moral values, social intercourse and political power of such places as the German Mennonite Mountain Lake, Minnesota (2000), Norwegian Lutheran Stoughton, Wisconsin (6100), Cajun Catholic Abbeville, Louisiana (14,000), Native American Gallup, New Mexico (16,000), Black Robbins, Illinois (9800), and numerous Mormon towns throughout the Western states. Whether or not these communities have a written covenant now or have had one at any time in their history, the unity of their *tacit assumptions* and *customary life styles* should be a legitimate concern for any newcomer. Some communities demand conformity, some presume it, some expect it, and some desire to overcome it. Within these towns the potential for a richly individual experience is high, but the potential for tension, ostracism and banishment is present, compounded for those strangers who are insensitive to cultural differences. It is likely that some of the more negative stereotypes of small town character originated in patterns of rejection of newcomers to such unified communities.

The expanded definition of "community covenant" includes not only these ethnically/religiously unified places, but theoretically any small town. My axiomatic assumptions are that a town *does* have an individual "character" and that the character is related to an "agreement" about what is most important to the town. This informal covenant is what the newcomer must cope with. Obviously the covenant is a majority or plurality agreement, and every community has non-subscribers to the covenant, ranging from opposition parties, to splinter groups, to independents. No town, even the strictest formal covenanted community, is consistent. Every New England Colonial Puritan town, from Plymouth on, had non-members.

But that is not important for my intended audience. A person's failure to adjust to a community is not brought on by the minorities. Minorities are easy for the newcomer to adjust to; all they require is tolerance, unless you are a member of the minority. It is the majority covenant that can make life tolerable or intolerable. Therefore it is

The way in which you encounter a town can imply the covenant. These buoyant messages on the railroad overpass in Two Harbors, Minnesota are for members only.

desirable to anticipate the covenant by reading its apparent signals. Forewarned is forearmed.[15]

The covenant is an agreement about what is important. Consider some "important things" in broad terms, and the concept will be clarified: PEOPLE, NATURE, PROGRESS, COMFORT, WORK, CHANGE, PRIVACY, HISTORY, COMMUNITY, DOMINANCE, YOUTH, SECURITY, MORALS, RECREATION, PROFIT, CLASS, UNIQUENESS, PRODUCTION, RIVALRY, GOD, EASE, SERVICE, EQUALITY, HEALTH, ACTIVITY, TOLERANCE, TERRITORY, and so on. A balanced community, like a balanced person, would probably value all of these, yet, at a given time, one or more things are valued more than the others, and this is a key to "life

Town covenants are dynamic, not static. Two Harbors has embarked upon a campaign of openness. The new Railroad Days summer festival includes this local author hawking his books beside local painters, ceramists and craftspeople. Town festivals often express real community values in consciously chosen symbols.

style."[16] Why this is true is a complicated matter of causes from historic tradition, from outside events, from social structure, from environment, and from individual leadership. The exploration of these and the verification of the hypothetical covenant are lifelong entertainments for thoughtful citizens; for the newcomer a quick reading is necessary.

Fortunately, towns usually have visual emblems of their covenant. These are of two types, the explicit, conscious symbol, and the implicit, unconscious or accidental signal.[17] Examples of the former are the statue of Paul Bunyan and his Blue Ox in Bemidji, Minnesota (12,000); the Corn Palace of Mitchell, South Dakota (14,000); the Court House in Buckhannon, West Virginia (7300)—or two thousand other county seats; the freeway billboards for New Boston, Texas (3700), which might be taken as the emblematic motto for many towns—*Large enough to serve you, Small enough to care;* "Petunia Boulevard" of Dixon, Illinois (17,000); the *two* bronze statues of Clermont, Iowa (600); the east and west entrance signs of Chandler, Oklahoma (2600)—"Chandler is Growing," "Chandler H.S. Home of the Lions"; the religious grotto of Dickeyville, Wisconsin (1100); the quaint welded steel pig statue in the courthouse square of Pittsfield, Illinois, or the immense purple-martinhouse pole in nearby Griggsville (1300).

One subtype of the conscious symbol is informal, like the town watertower whose graffiti exuberantly celebrates the local high school, or the railroad bridge over the highway into Two Harbors, Minnesota (4500), where bedsheets hang emblazoned with messages about high school reunions, social club picnics, birthdays or welcome-homes for individuals.

Another subtype of the conscious symbol is occasional. This is the town festival, such as the Apple Festival of Bayfield, Wisconsin (900), or the internationally famous Lumberjack Days of Hayward, Wisconsin (1500). There are undoubtedly dozens of these in every state. Some are well-known tourist attractions, but a great many are local only. I am indebted to one of my medical students for a valuable insight concerning these, especially since I formerly held the cynical view that these are the height of hokiness. Not so, he maintained;

rather they are like family reunions in which it is a best-foot-forward celebration of the ideal of the community, of what it wants to be; it is a celebration of sense of place, of uniqueness, of worth. It is at the other end of the scale from a low self-image, the adoption of small town stereotype and the shameful chagrin that townspeople often feel when they recognize their own provinciality.

How seriously are we to take these conscious symbols of the community covenant? Most certainly we should not interpret them at face value. They are emblematic only, and at the conscious level they are selected as positive symbols, although as observers from outside we may see them as sending messages that we read as warnings to stay away. The Babbitry of Chamber of Commerce booster signs, the falsification of historical fact in pageants, the painfully amateurish technical quality of statuary, the embarrassing choice of kitsch symbolism, the slickness of slogans or buildings that are clearly products of hired public relations experts, the adolescent rivalry with neighboring puberts and pygmies are often valid interpretations—in the mind of the beholder, which is where it matters for our audience. Furthermore, no symbol should be taken alone as an indicator of community values. And finally, it must always be borne in mind that not only are there minorities present, but that there are individuals in every house in town.

Nevertheless, there are two detailed studies of individual small towns that provide profound techniques for reading conscious symbols as serious and significant expressions of the small community. W. Lloyd Warner's five-volume study of "Yankee City" (Newburyport, Massachusetts, 16,000) ended with his 1959 *The Living and The Dead*, which includes more than one hundred pages analyzing the Tercentenary Pageant.[18] Most interesting is his examination of the community's manipulation of historical "realities" to support, sanction and justify the life styles and social structure of today's (circa 1940) town. It is, as Warner entitles the sixth chapter, "The Past Made Present and Perfect." This is not the place to recount this readable piece of interpretive sociology, but it is worth mentioning that he examines the manner in which certain historical periods are expanded in the pageant with reference to specific personages, and others are compressed, with historical citizens reduced to types. In addition, Warner studies the contemporary groups who prepared each tableau, inquiring into the social dynamics and motives of each. In brief, the symbols of a local pageant are not to be idly dismissed as contrived publicity or as self-deluding rationalization or as the naive antics of rustics cavorting upon the village green.

A more recent study of an individual town, "Appleton" (Paw Paw, Michigan, 3200) by the French-born anthropologist Hervé Varenne is the subject of *Americans Together, Structured Diversity in a Midwestern Town* (1977).[19] Varenne views Appleton like an anthropologist from a foreign culture examining a "primitive" community, and employing the structuralist approaches of Claude Lévi-Strauss.[20] The result is that Varenne sees this town not with "eyes that rove over tedious riddles solved long ago,"[21] but with the fresh puzzlement of one encountering an exotic society of strange ways and creeds. In doing so, he looks carefully at American small town *myths of origin*, such as that of the Farm Bureau! Combining these with autobiographies, with erroneous but nevertheless believed statements about local political organization, and with the creeds and rituals of several churches, Varenne, as a structuralist, searches for the universal common denominators that represent the essential glue that binds the diversity of small town and American life into a whole. The myths are the necessary mediators to make sense of the diametric poles of individualism and community.[22] This is heady stuff for non-anthropologists, though Varenne writes engagingly, but for our purposes it is enough to say that the carefully wrought creed-statements of social, political, economic and cultural groups—including those affixed to banners, billboards, letterheads, publicity folders and building facades—are worth scrutinizing for common meanings, regardless of how vapid each may seem. Before leaving this, one should also note Vidich and Bensman's *Small Town in Mass Society*, especially the chapter, "Springdale's Image of Itself." Here casual statements elicited in interviews are generalized into the covenant of "just plain folks."[23]

All of these are verbal studies—the overall picture of Vandalia, "Appleton," "Springdale," and "Quaker City" is like one received from a television set with a burned-out picture tube. This analogy, then, brings me to the second type of visual emblems of the covenant, those that are implicit, unconscious or accidental signals.

At a theoretical level, these can be designated as (1) size and centrality, (2) spatial relations and orientation, and (3) care and attention. My indebtedness here is to two books that are about cities rather than towns, Edmund N. Bacon's *The Design of Cities* (1974) and Grady Clay's *Close-Up: How to Read the American City* (1973),[24] both of which brilliantly and entertainingly educate the eye. Clay, in particular, invents two useful concepts, that of the *epitome district* and the *venturi*. Of the former, Clay says, "Special places in cities carry huge layers of symbols that have the capacity to pack up emotions, energy or history into a small place ... crammed with clues that trigger our awareness to the larger scene ..." and that "seldom stand still" for

The highest structure in a town may be an indicator of values and community priorities. The court house cupola is a dominant symbol in PawPaw, Michigan (although perspective distorts the higher water tower and lower shopping center sign).

The courthouse dome of Two Harbors, Minnesota has a low profile like the schools and churches of this town, suggesting a noncompetitive community covenant.

"the symbolic load is forever shifting." Of the latter, the *venturi* (a narrow tube in an automobile carburetor) he says, "This is the distinct pathway or network of paths along streets, sidewalks and corridors followed by central-city movers and shakers, influentials, wheelers and dealers, and hangers-on."[25] So much for theory and acknowledgements; on to some practical tools.

The tallest objects in a town cannot be ignored. From the Tower of Babel, to the Acropolis, to Notre Dame, to the Eiffel Tower to the skyline of Manhattan Island, height has equalled dominance—has equalled value. In many small towns, church steeples dominate, in others it is the grain elevator, in others a flag pole, the high school, an office building, the court house, a mansion on the hill. In still others, trees are the tallest objects, and in some, a hill, mountain or cliff. The suggestion in each instance is obvious and needs no further comment. A more ambivalent object is a water tower, and in most cases it would be overinterpretation to make anything of it. Nevertheless, it is almost sculptural in design, and despite its practical functionality, it is a visual magnet to the surrounding countryside. For a traveler looking for a gas station, a sandwich or a toilet, the water tower does state: here is a town. Some are anonymous—the town is "just plain folks"; others

The green of Colebrook, Connecticut is surrounded by buildings that express long continuity of New England town traditions. (Picture taken in 1971).

shout out their names in ten-foot high letters, and if a slogan is attached (often a superlative—the biggest, best, first, only) we know even more about pride and political unity. Accumulated graffiti have meaning, too. And there are styles of water towers. Many older suburbs disguised their utility in stone battlements, while go-getter modern communities have Hiroshima mushrooms that are painted a

swimming-pool aqua: the one with a beaux-arts aesthetic and a covenant with the past, the other a Bauhaus aesthetic and a covenant with
progress.

Centrality points to epitome districts. Probably the two most common American town designs are the Main Street and the central
square patterns.[26] These are artifacts of history, but the effects on life
styles dictated by traffic patterns have been profound. And even with
two later factors, the through highway and the shopping mall, the pace
of a central square town will be more leisurely than a Main Street
town, while a Main Street that culminates in a sharp turn or abrupt

*Reading the townscape for the tallest structure should take
in the whole context. The photograph of a mill in Del-
cambre, Louisiana tells only part of the story. The church
steeple in this Cajun town, along with the well-cared for
graveyard, should be considered, along with the masts and
booms of the shrimp fleet in a bayou lying only a few
hundred yards beyond.*

hill, the city park, or the high school facade will be cozier and more contained than one that carries the eye and the vehicle on to infinity. The former kind of Main Street, even if it bears the traffic of a highway, is likely to blend into a residential district, while the latter almost invariably dissolves visually into the car-lot, coin-op and franchise food strip if the town is relatively large and economically active, or if it is not, into a decay zone of dead filling stations and ma-and-pa grocery stores, abandoned warehouses and machine shops, and untenanted farm buildings. In short, containment of the retail commercial area maximizes pedestrianism and either prevents (or more likely) masks the fringe commerce.

"Venturis," those narrow beats that epitomize the power of the community are relatively easy to find in small towns. A coffee shop or lunch counter at breakfast (6:30–9:00 a.m.) or at coffee break bring together the commercial, legal, legislative, industrial and agricultural brokers who may or may not otherwise meet socially, or in church, or in political offices. The bank lobby is another venturi, as is the post office, or, sometimes, the right tavern. Over the years my medical students, who know their small hometowns, have overwhelmingly favored *the* restaurant in the morning as the center of significant action, and their intuition is supported by the close analysis of the restaurant as a major "behavior setting" for American small towns in Barker and Schoggen's *Qualities of Community Life* (1973).[27]

Spatial relations and orientation are interrelated with centrality. It is remarkable how many small towns are oriented to face the source of economic power, particularly in what Clay calls *strip* design: railroad, river and through-highway towns are especially clear examples. The river towns along the Mississippi, Ohio, and many other rivers have little choice, being backed up against a bluff, but many prairie towns face the grain elevators, loading docks, the railroad and the parallel highway. And in rural and small town America, "picture windows" frequently turn from the landscape and garden to face the highway or barnyard. This is a sign of a covenant with commerce.

Most, though not all, small towns have better and poorer residential districts, possibly even a Tom Thumb slum. Take note of the orientation of the poorer district to the better residential areas, the downtown, the highway, railroad and industrial plant. Sometimes democracy reigns, and the older, unfashionable, slightly shabby houses are interspersed among "colonials," "ramblers" and "split-levels." The explanation is fairly simple: the residents went to high school together, played ball together. One such person lived on the edge of town, with empty land around, but on water and gas mains. The newer houses express status by virtue of being newer houses rather than by being consistent with a protected neighborhood. This is a Midwestern and Northwestern phenomenon in large part, because of the absence of a tradition of distinctly separate classes with segregated territories, such as there are for black-white in the South, Yankee-immigrant in New England, Anglo-Chicano in the Southwest. Growth is another factor in residential democratization in towns: it isn't easy to establish exclusive neighborhoods if only a dozen houses are added in a decade, and, if the local economy is stable, the "shabby" homes are not vacated to be resold, or worse, rented to newcomers.

But that degree of democracy is not the norm. "Living on the other side of the tracks" is not an idle designation. The railroad is a barrier to easy intercourse and must divide two spaces and two orientations. Main Street can have the same effect. Natural barriers and natural attractions establish orientations that are rarely free of class differences. The riverfront will be shantytown or king's row, the mountainside will be hillbilly haven or doctors' demesne; any sign to the contrary is most likely not democracy but incomplete transition. The greatest rate of urban growth in recent years has been in small towns within commuting distance of major cities. Where there is rapid growth, there can be planned neighborhoods, and no planner ever planned democracy into the neighborhood. Developments with half-acre or more plots, self-consciously curving streets, and gateposts, archway, and wall indicate their inward orientation. The covenant is with security, social and economic.

The implicit, unconscious and accidental emblems of the covenant are dynamic, and thus the factors of size and centrality, spatial relations and orientation must be read in light of the apparent care and attention paid to the emblem. A booster billboard whose paint is fading, a painted-over WPA mural, a city park with no signs of use, a one-way Main Street oriented to visitors from only one direction, a hilltop mansion now a mortuary all point to lack of care or lack of attention and, more significantly, a shift in values. An informal symbol of community covenant is the residential front yard. The front yard is on the surface an entirely individual matter, but taken together yards become a community statement. In many towns, yard care is so highly valued that the person who does not meet the standard is shunned. Well-cared-for yards are also a signal of ownership, while many unkempt lawns suggest less permanent tenancy. And there are regional and ethnic differences, for example, the scraped and grassless yards of the Southeast. The clearest statements, of course, are those of yards enclosed by cyclone fences, with picture windows barred, as I have seen in some surburban small towns. The covenant is with physical security.

As an exercise, let me apply some of these techniques to reading four midwestern towns. Recently I drove through Clermont, Iowa (600), not stopping or pausing, and because of oncoming traffic, not being able to look closely as I passed. Approaching from the north, at the brow of the hill was a mansion and a historical marker for Governor Larrabee's Mansion park. Descending the hill, I was in a very small town with remarkable uniqueness. It had two tiny parks, each with a major bronze statue, one of the turn-of-the-century governor, the other of Abraham Lincoln. One of the parks I estimated to be about 200 square feet in size, but it was bounteous in peonies. The town had some abandoned red brick buildings, but there were definite signs of historic preservation activities. That is all I have to report, yet I postulated a covenant with history. Bronze full-length portrait statues have been out of style for close to half a century, so the covenant is not new; but renovating late nineteenth-century brick buildings is recent, so the covenant continues. The Governor's Mansion Park appeared to be a state project, but the peonies were not.

In Dixon, Illinois (17,000), I did stop, but only for the traffic lights on the highway. Dixon was busy—there were signs of an economically viable agricultural service center. The 1837 hotel had been renovated and showed signs of more practical use than as a museum. The Senior Citizens Drop-In Center had a high and proud profile. The past in

Dixon appeared to be valued for more than romantic nostalgia. But the main thing one notices in Dixon on a summer day is what Dixon wants noticed. Touted in signs at the end of town as *The Petunia City,* Dixon delivers the goods. The highway is named Petunia Boulevard, and it is not the only civic property planted with petunias: the street borders of private residences are also planted for a dozen or more city blocks. The petunias are not showy. They are widely spaced, not bunched profusely as one sees in professionally planned horticultural gardens. Furthermore, the petunias are plain, and few are double specimens or have candy-stripes or curly petals. They are plain, honest, grandma's petunias. I choose this example because it points out the importance of reading a small town in its regional context. I am something of a student of front yards, but any moderately observant transient through central Illinois would have noticed that aside from Dixonites, townspeople and farmers of the region do not landscape or decorate their yards. The yard of north central Illinois (at least from Peoria to

The approach to the main street of Griggsville, Illinois evokes the stereotype of "sleepy backwater town."

Dixon) appears to be a clipped portion of the prairie.[28] The contrast
with Iowa, Missouri, and Wisconsin, where at this time peonies,
bridal wreath, bleeding heart, lilies, pansies and petunias sang from
every yard, had been startling. Dixon's message was clear: it had
chosen to be a floral oasis, and it brought city and citizen together to do
this. Adding all the factors together, my dozen minutes of reading

*But just over the rise is the town's flamboyant purple mar-
tin house, smack in the middle of the street.*

Dixon recommended this starting point for closer reading: the covenant is with community.

I not only spent more time in Griggsville, Illinois (1300), but I approached it from three directions one June weekend. The initial view from the north frames a beautiful hillside cemetery with a livestock loading pen. Turning right onto the main street was not prepossessing. The business district was up on a small hill. The street was dusty, and many of the red brick commercial structures were empty, or in rundown condition. A tall tower of martinhouses was in the middle of the street, suggesting that birds were the main traffic in this moribund town.

My description is negative, but I intend it to be a warning not to trust first impressions. Indeed, I want it to cast a suspicious light upon my readings of Clermont and Dixon. I later approached Griggsville from the east, with a similar view. But the approach from the west provided a different picture. First, there is an active feed mill industry, and near it the county fair grounds, home of a very lively annual celebration and, I believe, harness racing. Turning toward the fair grounds, one comes upon a very well-kept city park with playground equipment, picnic tables and semiformal gardens. The homes are neat, many reflecting prosperity, and there is a mixture of old and new styles.

But most of all, the monumental birdhouse on main street is explained. Griggsville is the world's greatest commercial producer of martin houses! Moreover, from this business it has become a significant arts center. "Purple Martin Junction" contains a considerable number of connected purple railroad passenger cars, all air-conditioned and tastefully converted into a sales gallery for eighteenth and nineteenth century etchings, engravings, lithographs and water colors of birds, other animals and plants, and of specially commissioned contemporary nature studies, an art gallery of particularly choice nature art works, and a natural history museum. This is all an individual enterprise based upon the martinhouse industry, and I made no investigation into its interrelationship with the community. The moribund downtown is easily explained; it is the same story as can be witnessed in hundreds and hundreds of small towns. The automobile, declining railroads, the advent of supermarkets, luxury motels and discount stores combined to reduce the retail functions of many small towns to a skeleton. Griggsville's downtown moved to Pittsfield. The town covenant is ambiguous, but one would certainly start with the idea of residence.

The fourth and final town is Two Harbors, Minnesota (4500). My reason for using it as an illustration is to show that long acquaintance refines evidence as one tries to understand the complex organism that a small town must be. For a dozen years my home has been midway between Duluth and Two Harbors. My wife and I work in Duluth (100,000) and our patterns of consuming and service are probably about 60 percent in Duluth, 10 percent in Two Harbors, and 30 percent elsewhere (Minneapolis and other metropoli). Yet, in that dozen years, with weekly trips to Two Harbors for groceries, gasoline, lumber, hardware, gifts, clothing, medicine, our existence has only been acknowledged at the laundromat. This is doubly strange, for we have rather high profiles in the region, and several times each year one or the other of us will be featured in newspaper, television and radio stories. In addition, I have for sixteen years taught at the regional university, and many of the Two Harborites are former and current students. They will greet me at the University, but not in Two Harbors. In short, Two Harbors appears to be not "a friendly town," and almost a prototype for the sinister closed communities in popular melodramas that are guarding a heinous secret from prying outsiders. I should add one more factor before reading the town: there are broad regional differences in small town life styles, and although it is probably unprovable, it will be generally agreed that towns of the upper Midwest are not very outgoing; they tend to be reserved with strangers; and they do not maintain a conscious tradition of hospitality such as the South and West take such pride in. But these are our regional roots, too, and my wife and I are from small towns and share the ethnic heritage (both being German-Scandinavian) as well as the overall undemonstrativeness of the region. We are fully aware that we are not members of the Two Harbors community, nor have we had any reason to involve ourselves more directly than as casual though regular customers. Thus, our attitude is not cultural shock, rejection or disappointment; it is mild bemusement.

The ordinary approach to Two Harbors is on Highway 61, along the shore of Lake Superior—a portion of what Charles Kuralt has labelled one of "America's most spectacular roads."[29] The ordinary tourist undoubtedly presumes that the highway is main street. As with many towns that have endured highway widening or Dutch elm disease, this street has lost the bower-like character that provides the nostalgic association for American small towns. The railroad overpass may have one of the bedsheet announcements of reunions mentioned earlier, but otherwise the main emblem is encountered at the other end of town. This is a massive, cream-colored building, looking like a prison, or, as I long assumed, a major office building for iron ore shipping or, possibly, the headquarters for the National Forest Service. This building is also the first city sight for travelers from Canada, or for those coming down the county highway from the canoe country. It is Two Harbors High School, the second largest structure in Two Harbors. There is no sign of its identity. The largest structure is not immediately visible from any of the land approaches. This is the ore dock where immense ore carriers are loaded with taconite pellets brought by the industrial railroad from the Mesabi Iron Range.

To get to the dock, one must drive three blocks toward the lake, where the business street runs parallel to the highway. It is one block long, with a short spillover into the adjacent streets. It is a neat main street, attractive, quietly prosperous, active, but never crowded. A painted archway extends over one sidestreet, framing the harbor, lighthouse, oredock and the small outdoor railroad museum. "Welcome. Two Harbors harbor viewing," it says, and adds "museum, lighthouse, camping, trains, tugboat, golf." To the left is the American Legion Hall, to the right the Moose hall, soon to be vacated for a large modern building a block down the main street. A block away from this is the Masonic Lodge, and on the edge of town near the high school is the Veterans of Foreign Wars Post, the hospital, the civic and school recreational facilities, and the small area of new industrial and commercial development.

Another architectonic symbol: Two Harbors is county seat of Lake County. With 14,000 people the county is about three times the population size of Two Harbors, but in area Lake County is twice the size of

Rhode Island, and it is exceeded in size by only seven counties east of the Mississippi (plus four other Minnesota counties). The county is a wilderness of timber, lakes and rivers, except for the taconite processing plant at Silver Bay and the shipping at Silver Bay and Two Harbors. Yet the courthouse is hardly a statement of centrality or power. It is a handsome building with a low silver tesselated dome. Far from occupying a square or dominating main street, it is situated on a corner lot, back-to-back with one of the Lutheran churches, across from a vacant lot, kitty-corner to the small band-shell.

And finally, the churches of Two Harbors are numerous (there are ten in all), but none is taller than the neighboring trees, leaving as the tallest structure in town a five-story retirement high-rise. There are also several nursing facilities and a cooperative hospital.

The key to the covenant may be the cooperative medical program (a model in the state). The architectonic symbols of Two Harbors are non-competitive and inward-turning. The waterfront dock and railroad museum show in a dozen ways that this is a railroad town; the modest courthouse does not challenge the economic power. People are religious, but their churches are architecturally unassertive and non-competitive. A city of vistas, nothing major is oriented toward a vista, either natural or industrial. The civic tourist attractions are tucked away from the traffic flow, and the high school, situated on a hill and of a size that proclaims unequivocally a high value placed on education, has neither name nor portal for the transient visitor, but faces onto a quiet residential street. There are no imposing old mansions, there are no modern landscaped split-level estates, no "doctors' park." There is a co-op store, a co-op gas station, a co-op electric company, and co-op medical facility. There is a municipal liquor store, but no bars and no supper clubs. For a drink, one must go to the VFW or Moose Hall. In brief, Two Harbors is for members only, and the membership cards are issued at high school commencement. The covenant is internally egalitarian and externally exclusive. It is not "unfriendly," but the covenant is strong and self sufficient.

More could be said of a new economic progressivism since 1978 that has brought several new industries and has led to negotiations for liquor licenses for outside motel and restaurant interests, a "welcome" billboard outside the town, and the initiation of a summer pageant and a Main Street renovation. One could also introduce significant historical information about immigration, religion, and industry; and one could look more deeply into the power dynamics of city, county, merchants, and railroad. But these are, today, not to be read in the major symbols. The factors nonetheless illustrate again the complexity of small towns. As philosopher Albert Anderson has stated, the one essential ingredient of the City is *change*,[30] and as Grady Clay has said, epitome districts "seldom stand still," for "the symbolic load is forever shifting." Indeed, the definition of *covenant* can be extended to include its tenuousness. One must regard it as a temporary hypothesis, not a label, in assisting newcomers to develop original impressions about these unique, infinitely varied social organisms, the small towns of America.

In this essay, I have mentioned at least one hundred small towns, and I have suggested the individuality of each. My statements about them are vulnerable to at least a hundred different challenges, but not to the one that I have affixed to any town the stereotypes of "dull," "conformist," "uncultured," "provincial," "middle America" or "simple." My message, however, is simple: newcomers to small town residency must adjust to the *real* town, not to a stereotype. They will find that searching for the essence of the real town is a stimulating adventure.

NOTES

[1]Glenn V. Fuguitt and Calvin Beale, "Recent Trends in City Population Growth and Distribution," in *Small Cities in Transition: The Dynamics of Growth and Decline,* ed. Herrington J. Bryce (Cambridge, Mass.: Ballinger, 1977).

[2]Brian Berry, "Transformation of the Nation's Urban System: Small City Growth as Zero-Sum Game," in Bryce, *Small Cities in Transition.*

[3]On the currently dominant small town image, see Benjamin Stein, "The Electronic Elite Who Shape America's Taste," in *Popular Culture: Mirror of American Life,* ed. David Manning White and John Pendleton (Del Mar, Cal.: Publishers' Inc., 1977).

[4]Joseph P. Lyford, *The Talk in Vandalia: The Life of an American Town* (1964; rpt. New York: Harper and Row Colophon, 1965), p. 129.

[5]Populations are all based on "the 1970 census and latest available estimates" of the 1979 (55th ed.) *Rand McNally Road Atlas.* I provide them in part to keep me honest: many geographers, sociologists and urban planners seem to be over generous in their definition of a small town, following the census bureau in discounting towns of less

than 2500, and even placing the cutoff between "small" and "medium" at 150,000. See Seymour Sacks, "Changes in Manufacturing and Retailing Employment in Medium-Size Cities," in Bryce, *Small Cities in Transition*, p. 113. The preponderance of Midwestern examples is explained by my limiting my references to towns I have observed myself over the past decade.

[6]Lyford, pp. 41–51.

[7]Herrington J. Bryce, "Characteristics of Growing and Declining Cities," and Thomas Muller, "Fiscal Problems of Smaller Growing and Declining Cities," in Bryce, *Small Cities in Transition*.

[8]Arthur J. Vidich and Joseph Bensman, *Small Town in Mass Society: Class, Power and Religion in a Rural Community* (Princeton, N.J.: Princeton Univ. Press, 1958), pp. 79–86; 98–105; 292–314.

[9]Richard Lamb, *Metropolitan Impacts on Rural America* (Chicago: Univ. of Chicago Dept. of Geography Research Paper No. 162, 1975). Cf. Fuguitt and Beale.

[10]Werner Z. Hirsch, "The Coming Age of the Polynucleated Metropolis," in Bryce, *Small Cities in Transition*, especially pp. 277–81.

[11]Bureau of Census, *Statistical Abstract of the United States*, 99th ed. (Washington, D.C.: GPO, 1978), p. 23; Cf. Fuguitt and Beale.

[12]Page Smith, *As a City Upon a Hill: The Town in American History* (New York: Knopf, 1966). Chapters 1, 2 and 14 are particularly relevant.

[13]Smith, pp. 6–7, 17–20; see also p. 44.

[14]*Farm Report: The Year of the Soybean*, The Farm: Summertown, Tenn. [1978?].

[15]The potential conflicts can result from gross or subtle differences, and at times superficial gross differences make for easier adjustment. A white Roman Catholic family might be accepted more comfortably into a black Alabama town than that of a Northern urban black, while a Sioux Indian might fit into a German Catholic village better than a new German immigrant would. The broad spectrum of sensitivity required for anticipating and understanding irritating differences is probably beyond anyone's scope. Historical national rivalries may be significant in an unspoken source of conflict, as with English-Irish, Swedish-Norwegian, French-German, Chippewa-Sioux, and Union-Confederate. Changes in the homeland or New World history cause people with an ostensibly identical heritage to behave according to quite different social and psychological premises, as with Quebec French and European French, Germans who lived through the Nazi regime and earlier immigrants, American blacks and Africans, and so on. Religious differences, such as high and low-church Episcopalian, American and Wisconsin Synod Lutheran, Roman Catholic and Polish National Catholic, "Salt Lake City" and "Independence" Mormon appear to be absurdly trivial to outsiders. One could go on endlessly, including even intercity sports rivalries and wordless "proxemic" tensions. See Edward T. Hall, *The Hidden Dimension* (New York: Doubleday, 1966).

[16]"Life Style" is handily defined in Saul D. Feldman and Gerald W. Thielbar's *Life Styles: Diversity in American Society* (Boston: Little, Brown, 1972) as (a) a group phenomenon (b) pervading many aspects of life (c) implying a central life interest and (d) differing according to sociologically relevant variables, pp. 1–3.

[17]I have made deliberate use of three terms that are near synonyms in common usage. A *symbol* is understood simultaneously as thing and as meaning, a *signal* is the thing, whose meaning is not necessarily understood. See W. Lloyd Warner, *The Living and the Dead: A Study of the Symbolic Life of Americans* (New Haven: Yale Univ. Press, 1959), pp. 107–13, and pp. 212–21, which is particularly relevant to the idea of convenant. An *emblem* is a more ambiguous literary term, being suggestive of associations, connotations, surplus meaning.

[18]Warner, pp. 107–225.

Fred E. H. Schroeder

[19]Hervé Varenne, *Americans Together, Structured Diversity in a Midwestern Town* (New York: Teachers College Press, Columbia Univ., 1977).
[20]Varenne mercifully reserves theoretical observations for the "Post face," pp. 212–33.
[21]The line is from Thomas Hardy's poem "Neutral Tones."
[22]Varenne, pp. 29–35, 132.
[23]Vidich and Bensman, pp. 29–45.
[24]Edmund N. Bacon, *The Design of Cities* (New York: Viking, 1974). Grady Clay, *Close Up: How to Read the American City* (New York: Praeger, 1973).
[25]Clay, pp. 38,53.
[26]See, for example, Edward T. Price, "The Central Courthouse Square in the American County Seat," *Geographical Reivew*, 58 (Jan. 1968), 30–60.
[27]Roger G. Barker and Phil Schoggen, *Qualities of Community Life* (San Francisco: Jossey-Bass, 1973), pp. 8–11.
[28]For a broad view, see David Lowenthal, "The American Scene," *Geographical Review*, 58 (Jan. 1968), 61–88. More specifically, see my "The Democratic Yard and Garden" in *Outlaw Aesthetics; Arts and the Public Mind* (Bowling Green, Oh.: Popular Press, 1977), pp. 94–122.
[29]Charles Kuralt, "A Guide to America's Most Beautiful Roads," *Family Circle*, 17 July 1979, p. 41.
[30]Albert A. Anderson, unpublished paper (Philosophy Dept., Clark Univ., Worcester, Mass.).

Architectural Preservation in Natchez, Mississippi:
A *Conception of Time and Place*

MICHAEL FAZIO

Today the South seems to interest many Americans, some for political or economic reasons, others for reasons related to leisure time, travel and exploration. Architectural preservation has, I think, contributed significantly to this interest. And in one location, the former cotton-boom town of Natchez, Mississippi, preservation has developed into a major industry, if not a way of life. I shall focus in this article upon the Natchez Pilgrimage of Homes, a yearly celebration centered around historic architecture. It is a phenomenon which reveals much about the architectural past and present in a small Southern town. It may also contain a message about the future of the preservation move-ment—in Natchez and similar communities around the country.

Natchez may perhaps best be understood by looking at the four different periods of its past and present: the antebellum era, when the great plantations and mansion houses were built; Reconstruction, during which time the entire plantation economy collapsed and the great dwellings (like Faulkner's Southern women characters) were "made into ghosts";[1] the early twentieth century, specifically around 1930 when the Natchez Pilgrimage of Homes began; and the present day, which is marked by the general characteristics of any small town. Natchez's story is instructive for what it reveals about preservation problems and strategies for small town preservation.

Interesting not only as a historic artifact, Natchez is also remarkable for the attention that its old homes seem to evoke. This attraction may be attributed, perhaps, to what I would term the "Southern qualities." The South represents a distinct and fascinating region, possessed of an integral and unifying element—a sense of place—and seems to man-ifest an air of mystery, a certain benign countenance of the enigmatic

136

or inexplicable. Natchez appears to have tapped both of these resources.

Natchez prospered during the first half of the nineteenth century
because of surrounding deposits of rich, cotton-producing alluvial
soil. Absentee ownership was the rule among Mississippi River plan-
ters; consequently, Natchez served as a pleasure village for plantation
masters who made their fortunes in the back country but maintained
their mansion houses in town. When the Civil War came, these
wealthy landowners represented a conservative minority who had the
most to lose if the war effort failed; and they joined the radical,
war-minded Democrats only with great reluctance. Thus when Federal troops eventually entered Natchez, they were actually welcomed
by much of the population. General P. T. Beauregard wrote with
incredulity that "the political condition of your section of the country
is astonishing."[2] Perhaps it was for this reason that the town of Natchez
suffered little damage from hostile action. Nevertheless, with the
complete demise of the plantation system after the war, the Southern
economy collapsed, and Natchez entered into a sort of comatose state,
forgotten by most of the outside world.

Not until the 1930s did Natchez experience renewed economic
vitality as a function of the general industrial migration southward.
During these years, the town began its Pilgrimage of Homes tours,
which also elicited an investment of time and money from outsiders.
The pilgrimage was an immediate success. Although no simple explanation for it is apparent, I would offer the hypothesis that the
qualities of the sense of place and the Southern mystery chiefly
account for this success.

Sense of place pertains at one scale to regions, at another to small
communities, but always to tangible, local characteristics and to richness of visual and symbolic imagery. Certainly any geographical entity can lay claim to its own sense of place; but the South, I would
insist, possesses along with a number of obvious native characteristics, such as extremes of climate and flora and the lingering
presence of the Civil War, one singular trait. David M. Potter, writing
in the *Yale Review*, has described both the obvious and singular:

  . . . the Southern theme has held an unusual appeal for the people of the

South because of their peculiarly strong and sentimental loyalty to Dixie as their native land, and for Americans outside the South because of the exotic quality of the place and because it bears the aura of a Lost Cause. . . .

But it seems unlikely that . . . the South . . . could hold so much . . . popular attention . . . if [it] were not also an *enigma* [italics mine].[3]

To some observers, like H. L. Mencken, the South has mirrored nothingness; but to others, Potter again suggests, the region stands as a sphinx that "has seemed to hold a secret, an answer to the riddle of American life."[4] One wonders how this can be. How can the South, once a geographical reprobate, the target of the most vitriolic abolitionist furies, now exhibit a benign presence and hold promise as the goal of cultural pilgrimages?

To begin with, the South has experienced a visual purification; the extant trappings of the slave-holding past are now exhibited as a laundered and carefully packaged and marketed visage. Slave quarters are usually missing; in fact, the whole plantation substructure has typically disappeared—by design or neglect, as well as by Yankee destruction, leaving only the grand image of the great house on the hill. Another explanation of the South's newly found attractiveness probably lies in the region's tradition of rural simplicity. Certainly the antebellum economic foundation, built as it was upon the exploitation of men and land, remains an unfortunate fact of history, but to many observers the South still embodies the simple Jeffersonian virtues of agrarianism. And a strong case can be made for the existence of an important man-nature relationship in the South for blacks as well as for whites.

As a result of this homage to the land, Southern culture remains personal and maintains a distinctive tempo; in the process it evokes what Potter calls a "persistent, haunting nostalgia."[5] Perhaps the source of this nostalgia never really existed as many imagine it, but to a significant public the Old South represents a place that they at least want to believe existed—not sordid and exploitative—but a sophisticated folk culture (a built-in contradiction), the somewhat mysterious agrarian civilization that left as its residue the great antebellum houses. Visitors to the South today can find evidence of either the quite real and distinctive lifestyle of the antebellum period or conjure up an even more individual and romantic image from their own imaginations, using the remaining architecture as a setting.

Such a romantic interpretation is nothing new however. The Old South was viewed just as romantically, if not more so, by its own citizens, even though these same citizens saw themselves as worshipers at the shrine of classicism. Among the many ploys used by the antebellum South to legitimize slavery was a fantastic attempt to identify with the slave-holding civilizations of classical antiquity; romanticism and classicism became curiously mixed in the Southern mind. The famous Civil War ranger John Mosby sent a well-known letter home from the front asking for a schizophrenic array of classical and romantic volumes from his library: Plutarch's *Lives*, Macaulay's *History*, Sir Walter Scott's novels and poems, Shakespeare, Byron, and Hazlitt's *Life of Napoleon*.[6]

The most productive aspect of such confused antebellum classicism emerged not as orderly classical thought, but as romantic, classicized architecture. The Greek Revival, tucked in and pristine in the Midwest and in New England, was galvanized in the South by the extravagant colors, shapes, and fragrances of the landscape, and by the hot, languid, almost stupefying climate, into an outburst of galleries and colonnades and great shuttered windows, an apparition like some strange, hybridized Southern plant.

After 1830 and the final, irreversible confirmation of slavery as the basis for Southern life, the classic-romantic balance began to swing toward an ever stronger romanticism. During this period, plantation owners, like feudal lords, lived the existence of a resuscitated European aristocracy. Their lifestyle might today be called decadent, but they considered themselves men of action; they lived in and for the present. They made history as they saw it; the fire eater William L. Yancey exclaimed in his typically lofty rhetoric: "Our poetry is our lives: our fiction will come when truth has ceased to satisfy."[7] Greek Revival architecture in its transmuted Southern form provided the stage on which this outlandish, dramatic, mythic lifestyle could be lived or played out.

Ultimately the defense of slavery led to the complete romanticizing of the Southern psyche. As the "peculiar institution" came under increased pressure, Southern intellect turned more and more inward; and sometime in the years just prior to the war, a Southern consciousness of the past emerged, a consciousness that would be greatly heightened during Reconstruction. Southerners for the first time sought to stop the clock and to glorify the status quo, and ultimately to reverse the flow of time altogether. Preservation in the most general sense began as an attempt to preserve an archaic way of life on collision course with the demands of a modern world, and only later focused on architecture. The entire antebellum Southern experience lasted barely a generation; consequently, there was not time to consider preserving monuments and barely enough time to build them. Preservation of the physical past eventually occurred as a result of passivity, when no money and little energy were available to modify the built environment. Architecture was ultimately preserved simply because it was ignored.

The metamorphosis from antebellum to Reconstruction mentality can be witnessed through literature written about the South, specifically in the works of two novelists, William Faulkner and Sarah Orne Jewett. In his novel of the antebellum South, *Absalom, Absalom!* Faulkner describes Thomas Sutpen, the mysterious figure who arrived in Yoknapatawpha County with nothing but "a horse and two pistols" and seeking respectability—"a home, position: a wife and family which, being necessary to concealment, he accepted along with the rest of respectability as he would have accepted the necessary discomfort and even pain of the briers and thorns in a thicket if the thicket could have given him the protection he sought."[8]

The "home" or, more literally, the house emerges as an important image. Sutpen brought along with him a band of slaves, "a herd of wild beasts he had hunted down singlehanded," and a "French architect who looked like he had been hunted down and caught in turn by the negroes." The architect with the "Latin face" and "flowered waist coat and hat" lived on the site for two years: "The architect . . . [with] his expression of grim and embittered amazement lurked about the environs of the scene with his air something between a casual and bitterly disinterested spectator and a condemned and conscientious ghost . . . [amazed] . . . General Compson said, not at the others and what they were doing so much as at himself, at the inexplicable and incredible fact of his own presence."[9]

The Frenchman endured, and he designed and built for Sutpen a mansion second in size only to the courthouse itself. Sutpen exemplified the crudity and ignorance of the frontier; he had neither background nor position; he came seeking both, along with the proper architectural setting for his new life. Like most aspiring plantation owners, he sought a ready made past. Property made a gentleman and architecture was the ultimate embellishment of property.

Faulkner's Old Testament specter of the antebellum South stands in sharp contrast to the New Testament image presented by such Reconstruction novelists as Sarah Orne Jewett, a New Englander writing in the 1880s. The example of a New Englander serves to show the universality of the new image of the South which evolved in Reconstruction thought and literature about the region. Jewett concentrates on the "luckless post-bellum patricians" and the tragedies of war. She investigates sympathetically the vision of past glories, shattered grandeur, and nostalgia which enveloped the region after the war. Her message is that laws and military force will not unite North and South; rather, it will be love and understanding. She focuses on "indigenous scenes, characters and customs, and native perspicuity and understanding."[10] She waxes emotional about her subject, trying to turn back the clock and discover a beautiful image.

Jewett was only one among many writers who took up this subject after Appomattox. Northern opinion was so thoroughly conquered by the image of a new acquiescent South that polemicists such as the abolitionist, Judge Albion W. Tourgee, writing in 1888, would say in exasperation: "Not only is the epoch of the War the favorite field of American fiction today, but the Confederate soldier is the popular hero."[12] The South had been purged of slavery, and to much of the populace, especially in the North, a new phenomenon, both grand and menacing, moved to mid-stage: industrialization. Consequently, the South came to represent a place, according to Paul H. Buck, where "nostalgic Northerners could escape the wear and tear of expanding industry and growing cities and dwell in a Dixie of story books which had become the Arcady of American tradition."[12]

Agrarian anti-industrial sentiment after the War was certainly one reason for the change in Northern temper, but the emerging image of the South as a unique place was another. The common cause in the South had made of the once heterogeneous complex of hamlets and isolated agricultural empires a monolithic culture. The South was seen from the outside not only as a holdover from simpler times but also as a mysterious, special entity, a repository of ancient virtues and of regional identity.

The change in the role of women during this period also related directly to the later development of the preservation movement in the South. Women had not lost the War directly; they had watched it being lost. Most of them had not found the enemy at hand and were, consequently, left with unvented frustrations, perhaps more so than the men, who at least had been involved in direct confrontation. Women sought ways to alleviate their remorse and maintain a continuing sense of hostility and pride before their conquerors. Confederate Decoration Day represents an early result.

Women also went to work. The lives of leisure which many had known vaporized, and women were forced to meet the challenge of simple day to day existence. They found a means to idealize the past without interfering with the practices of the present. Women took the lead in the preservation of their Southern heritage and would eventually find in architecture their greatest opportunity for a glorification of the past, one that would also turn a profit. In the case of the Natchez Pilgrimage, the statement would be made by the women themselves that "the remarkable success of this adventure is its justification,"[13] a pragmatic, not romantic statement.

By 1900 the South, with the help of the literary community, had fabricated from the scraps of the Confederacy an imagery of simple beauty, warmth, and grace—no small task! The region had succeeded, as W. J. Cash says in *The Mind of the South*, "in creating a world which, if it was not made altogether in the image of the old world, half-remembered and half-dreamed, shimmering there forever behind the fateful smoke of Sumter's guns, was yet sufficiently of a piece with it in essentials to be acceptable, a world which by and large would serve as a reasonably proper garment for its mind."[14]

The stage was set for rebirth of an awareness about the South, not only as a literary creation, but also as a tangible, approachable reality. America suffered through two more wars and a depression. The Spanish American War served to reunite the divided armies, and World War I, while completing this amalgamation, raised the level of American consciousness of itself and of its heritage. The depression, which rocked every institution of the country in 1929, made romance and nostalgia a universal vision and made defeat, albeit economic defeat, understandable to all of America.

People sought relief from these dilemmas. Many architectural solutions of the period played a part in this search: Moorish and Byzantine movie theatres where ticket holders could, for a few hours, live out a fantasy, the outpouring of the fanciful, folklore style of PWA artwork in post offices and train stations throughout the country, the popularity of the restoration of such pseudo historical worlds as Colonial Williamsburg. Natchez's star as a part of this mystical search was again in ascendance. Circumstances were right for displaying a born-again version of the Old South in the guise of brooding, purified, resurrected antebellum architecture. The yearning for romance, for dream, for retreat from reality provided the foundation for the success of the Natchez Pilgrimage of Homes.

In 1927 the garden club movement began in Athens, Georgia. By 1929 garden clubs were active in Alabama, and the movement continued to spread. A State Garden Club Convention was scheduled in Natchez, Mississippi, for the spring of 1931. Depending upon the source quoted, homes were chosen to be shown instead of gardens either because far-sighted women recognized that, while no worthwhile gardens existed, the homes themselves were extraordinary, or because an early frost arrived, killing the tender spring foliage and forcing the selection of alternate displays. Already, the truth here remains elusive and ambiguous. This ambiguity resulted in no small part from the fact that two rival garden clubs ultimately emerged in town. The Natchez Garden Club was formed earliest and remained the lone standard bearer until 1937, when the Pilgrimage Garden Club was created. The reasons for the organization of the second club vary, from Mrs. Balfour Miller's euphemistic description of "a division

of interest" to Harnett Kane's suggestion that among the many motives
for the split were "personalities and especially money."[15]

A thinly-veiled peaceful coexistence of the two factions was maintained until 1941 when antagonisms escalated into a full-scaled legal
dispute and were ultimately aired before a judge. Harnett Kane nar-
rates the situation in a traditionally Southern storytelling fashion:

> Thick faced deputies started out, nailing notices to Georgian doors. One
> chatelaine, not knowing what was happening, saw the Law coming up the
> walk and mistook it for a tourist. She dropped him a deep bow, "and then he
> handed me an injunction!" That, sir, was hardly the act of a gentleman.
> Certain ladies scurried around town, fleeing justice; and rode to the Devil's
> Punchbowl, where bandits of the Natchez trace used to hide out when the
> law was tailing them. Town officials, pressed to "do something," stared at
> the ground. The mayor found he had business in New York and left for a
> week; many husbands wished they could follow him.[16]

Counter suits followed. Fortunately all litigation was eventually dismissed and after the hiatus of the Second World War, an agreement
was reached in 1947 leading to a joint pilgrimage. Such a cooperative
arrangement continues today.

The pilgrimage has become an extraordinary economic success and
has spawned many other similar events across the country. In the
process, the Natchez garden clubs have generated monies to maintain
and restore properties which would have otherwise gone to ruin, and
the argument could be forcefully made that the preservation movement and its energies have saved the entire town. Accomplishments
include building restorations, the placing of numerous individual
structures on the National Register of Historic Places, the establish-
ment of legislatively controlled historic districts subject to architectural review, and a county-wide historic resource inventory. One
entire section of the city has been submitted to the National Register
of Historic Places and more work is underway on the designation of
other similar areas.

As interesting as the physical accomplishments of the preservation
movement in Natchez have been the attitudes prevalent among the
organizers and sympathizers. These attitudes reflect an awareness of a
sense of place, a consciousness of mystery, and especially an understanding of the public's thirst for romanticism and nostalgia. For

example, Mrs. Balfour Miller, describing her address to the opening banquet of the Federation of Garden Clubs in 1931 said: "I asked our guests to take themselves back in imagination one hundred years and visualize the grandeur of a bygone era as they looked at our houses on the tour; and I asked them to dream with us the dreams of the future Natchez restored to its former glory." Another citizen described the pilgrimage as "mute evidence of the halycon days of romance and beauty." Even the choice of the term "pilgrimage" is revealing.

The prevalence today of a renewed romantic spirit among Southerners and Northerners—among all of us, in fact—popularized places and events such as the Natchez pilgrimage in which we are able to pretend and dream and enjoy ourselves amidst a mythical setting (Disney World being the consummate example). This amusement seems harmless enough as long as fantasy does not become a surrogate for truth, but such a danger exists in Natchez. Antebellum history is not being accurately presented there and cannot be until a more complete display of all types of plantation buildings and mansion compounds exists. Providing such a display will of course necessitate a detailed study of the structures. This recommendation is not meant as some accusation of an architectural original sin. The peculiar institution has been disposed of completely, and no one needs to be chastised for slavery's existence. But blacks and whites alike deserve to understand more completely this ignominious corner of history, however unsavory. Natchez could benefit from such a broad architectural consciousness and the individual homes would not suffer as a result; an abundance of romance would still remain.

Likewise the element of mystery, inherent in so much of Southern culture, can withstand a slight raising of the veil. Filling in a few important blanks will not erase the enigma and perhaps will only serve to deepen it. Too many thoughtful individuals from all parts of the country continue to reflect upon this basic Southern quality to imagine that behind the puzzling facade exists only a vacuous wasteland. A region that today commands multi-volume histories, stacks of college textbooks, quarterly journals, a virtual library of monographic studies, and one of the world's richest literary legacies need not worry about the substantiality of its cultural base.

Sense of place should also be nurtured as a Southern resource. A recent editorial in *Architectural Record* stresses a "growing conviction that in regional characteristics and traditions and images are the roots of a contemporary architecture to which people will respond."[7] This statement reflects broad contemporary sentiments; regionalism is a topical issue not only because it is a historical conception but a potential solution to contemporary problems. And small towns like Natchez seem to be in an ideal position to exploit this trend. Small towns have special qualities; they are not microcosms of large cities. As a corollary, small towns have unique problems, some of which are directly related to preservation.

Vidich and Bensman in *Small Town in a Mass Society,* suggest some of these small town qualities. They point out that while cities are seen as impersonal and lonely, small towns embody friendliness and intimate social contact. When asked about the qualities of their small towns, these authors say that citizens mention honesty, fair play, truthfulness, good neighborliness, helpfulness, sobriety, and even clean living. Small towns, according to their study, seem to be places where "everybody knows everybody," where people are community minded and where people can get a "sense of roots."[18]

Current periodical literature has also stressed the renewed interest of Americans in small towns. People are moving back, and this shift represents an about-face in the American tradition of urbanization. An essay in an issue of *Saturday Review* dedicated entirely to "The American Hometown" suggests that "the more progressive a society becomes, the less the people flock toward traditional symbols of progress. As a society advances ... economic features are not as important to them as human values, pleasures, and physical surroundings."[19] The Natchez preservation movement has capitalized upon these "hometown" attributes.

Preservation in Natchez has succeeded in its primary mission. Buildings have been saved and, as a result, at least part of an earlier way of life has been put on display. In the process, the economic viability of the town has been assured. If a single dilemma in the Natchez circumstance were to be identified, it might well be the elitist nature of preservation activities. Ron Miller, a historian active in

Natchez, has said that "unfortunately the remarkable and commenda-
ble efforts of the women have resulted locally in a feeling that preservation is a sexually and socially exclusive activity."[20] In all fairness,
however, this feeling seems to be symptomatic of preservation activities across the country and not just a local phenomenon. Furthermore, the roots of the dominance of women in Southern preservation
reach back to Reconstruction, as has been discussed. Still, it would
seem that preservation as a concerted effort directed toward the improvement of the quality of the overall environment and aimed at a
broad cross section of the populace remains a desirable goal.

Small towns like Natchez display settings which have not been
"overwhelmed by mass media, mass culture, mass marketing and
mass society."[21] As a result, small towns have often lain outside the
mainstream of power and priorities of big government. Small towns
have preservation problems which are unique and are just as serious
in their own way as the dilemmas faced in larger urban areas. However, these problems have often been ignored at state and federal
levels. As Carol J. Galbreath has written, small towns lack huge
staffs of "trained community service personnel, planning and admin-
istrative coordination, lucrative economic bases and access to capital,
consumer marketing systems, [and] local organizations to influence
decision making."[22] Natchez has succeeded in preserving its heritage
largely on its own, partly because of the nature of local society but
partly out of sheer necessity: large cities have received the lion's share
of grant monies which might have been used for preservation purposes in small towns.

Despite all their adversities, small towns generally have endured.
In the process they have begun to recognize that preservation can be a
key to their survival. Small towns simply cannot absorb or finance
enormous change. Small towns must remain largely stable or, put
more positively, must seek controlled, desirable, incremental growth
in order to maintain their identities. Historic preservation strengthens
this identity and its underlying cultural systems by making older,
familiar buildings serve contemporary uses and by encouraging a
creative reinterpretation of traditional building forms in terms of
modern technology and needs. The resulting visual unity enhances

the sense of continuity, strengthens the feeling of belonging, and establishes an overall sense of place. Historic preservation in this way can and often must "be the point of entry for constructive change in social, political, economic, and cultural systems of small towns."[23]

Small towns like Natchez have not succumbed to superficial modernization, but rather have retained and even marketed their special historical environments, their singular identities, their sense of place. Today with the South's growing social, economic, and political visibility tourists have become more curious than ever about the lingering mysteries of the region. The Natchez Pilgrimage of Homes gives Americans an opportunity to investigate the Southern mystery for themselves and to enjoy the experience. Natchez and other similar small towns across the South (and the nation) can and should continue to use preservation as a way to understand the past, not just selected vignettes but all of it, and as a way to involve a broad spectrum of the populace in the management of their present environment—to create a sense of place and a sense of control and enjoyment of the future as part of the overall Southern and American experience.

NOTES

[1]William Faulkner, *Absalom, Absalom* (1936; rpt. New York: Modern Library, 1951), p. 12. Here Mr. Compson says to Quentin: "Years ago we in the South made our women into ladies, then the war came and made the ladies into ghosts."

[2]As quoted in William Banks Taylor, *King Cotton and Old Glory* (Natchez, Miss.: Ransom Rombo, 1977), p. 45.

[3]David M. Potter, "The Enigma of the South," *Yale Review*, 51 (Autumn 1961), 142.

[4]Potter, p. 143.

[5]Potter, p. 151.

[6]Clement Eaton, *The Mind of the Old South* (Baton Rouge: Louisiana State Univ. Press, 1967), pp. 249–50.

[7]Eaton, p. 239.

[8]Faulkner, pp. 14 and 16.

[9]Faulkner, pp. 16 and 38.

[10]Richard Carey, *Sarah Orne Jewett* (New York: Twayne, 1962), pp. 129, 18, 19.

[11]Paul H. Buck, *The Road to Reunion* (Boston: Little, Brown, 1937), p. 234.

[12]Buck, p. 235.

[13]Mrs. George Wilson Newell and Charles Compton, *Natchez and the Pilgrimage* (n. p.: Southern Publishers, 1935), p. 39.

[14]W. J. Cash, *The Mind of the South* (New York: Alfred A. Knopf, 1941), p. 216.

[15]The historical development of the Natchez Pilgrimage of Homes has not been studied in any systematic way. Substantiated factual information is simply lacking, but the various available sources do seem to project a clear and fairly consistent account of

the meaning of preservation in the town. I have drawn here upon the following sources: Katherine Grafton Miller, *Natchez Is a Fairy Story* (Natchez: Pilgrimage Garden Club, 1974) and *Natchez of Long Ago and the Pilgrimage,* a short book by the same author (no date or place of publication given); Harnett T. Kane, *Natchez on the Mississippi* (New York: Bonanza Books, 1947) Newell and Compton's *Natchez and the Pilgrimage.*

[16]Kane, pp. 346–47.

[17]Walter Wagner, "Some Random Reflections on Regionalism," *Architectural Record,* 163 (April 1978), p. 13.

[18]Arthur J. Vidich and Joseph Bensman, *Small Town in Mass Society: Class, Power and Religion in a Rural Community,* rev. ed., (Princeton: Princeton Univ. Press, 1968), p. 29.

[19]"The American Hometown," *Saturday Review,* 26 Nov. 1977, p. 10.

[20]Ronald Miller, "Historic Preservation in Natchez, Mississippi," *Antiques,* 111 (March 1977), p. 539.

[21]Carol J. Galbreath, "Small Town Preservation—A Systematic View," *Historic Preservation,* 27 (April-June 1975), 12. Many of the ideas in this closing section have been summarized from this article.

[22]Galbreath, p. 15.

[23]Galbreath, p. 15.

The Small Town Editor:
Guardian of Respectability

GERALD K. WELLS

Until the mid-nineteenth century, American literature represented the small town as an idyllic retreat from the realities of life. Following the example set forth in Oliver Goldsmith's "The Deserted Village," early American poets Philip Freneau and Timothy Dwight and later writers of sentimental fiction testified to the existence of a place in which innocence and communal harmony were the normal habits of life. In this remote hideaway the battered traveler of life could escape the pressures of the contemporary world. As long as writers such as these used the village setting as a means of seeking the simplicity of an indefinite past period of time, the nostalgic tone, similar to that of Goldsmith's poem, remained the dominant mood of the village tradition.[1]

After the Civil War, however, American realistic writers turned from the sentimentalized portrait of the small town and its people to a sharp, critical attack upon American village life. Guided by their observations and experiences among provincial people, these writers noticed wide discrepancies between the former accounts of these homogeneous, democratic little societies and the patterns of social behavior they found operating around them; and, in their writings, they attempted to present a more accurate, often satiric, picture of provincial life.

In reviewing the changing attitude of late nineteenth century authors toward the small town, literary critics have often centered their attention on a small number of writers, such as Edgar Lee Masters and Sinclair Lewis, in whose works the methods of critical realism are most apparent. Unfortunately, this approach leaves the impression

150

that these new attitudes toward the small town were the creation of modern iconoclasts attempting to destroy a tradition which, until the twentieth century, had remained unchallenged. The "revolt phase" in American literature, however, traces its roots back to the period of American Realism when writers turned from idealizing the past and began writing literature based upon their observations and experiences. Following the guidance of such national literary figures as William Dean Howells, these writers sought to immerse themselves in the conflicts and tensions of the contemporary American milieu and relate faithfully what they had actually seen and felt about the life around them. Drawing upon the scientific methods of observation, analysis, and classification, and upon the Emersonian preference for the commonplace, they attempted "to narrow the gap between fiction and non-fiction, to write fiction that was largely autobiographical," that dealt with everyday occurrences in American life.[2] Thus, the attacks upon the American small town in the first decades of the twentieth century were the culmination of attitudes, ideas, and observations already deeply embedded in American literary tradition.

Leadership of the revolt movement came from the Midwestern writers and the principal subjects of their assaults were the carefully ordered, highly stratified midwestern towns. Chief among the targets in these towns were the dominant middle class citizens, composed mainly of business and professional people, a group Sinclair Lewis labels "the oligarchy of respectability."[3] These persons held the upperclass positions—or had access to them—and, in most towns, their cultural tastes and values set the social patterns for the entire community. In attacking the middle class, therefore, these writers hoped to expose the main corrupting influences in village life and, ultimately, to bring about the changes they felt were needed in the social consciousness of provincial people.

In their fiction realistic writers tended to treat the middle class as a group rather than single out a particular business or profession for special attention. When members of the class, such as the lawyer Squire Gaylord of Howells's *A Modern Instance* or Dr. Kennicott of Sinclair Lewis's *Main Street*, emerge from the class to become fully realized characters, they are less valuable to a small town study in revealing characteristics of their profession than as individuals in their own right or spokesmen for middle-class provincial values. Aside from the minister and the teacher, neither of whom typifies the middle class, the only professional or business type to receive extensive treatment was the village editor. As a result, a careful look at the village editor provides insight both into the profession itself and into the values, tastes, and social mores of middle class life in the American small town.

Within this powerful middle class, the village editor held a unique position. Generally he had been reared in the town, educated in the local school system and the town's newspaper office, and worked into the editor's chair through a long apprenticeship. If having remained in the town most of his life restricted his understanding of the outside world, his wide reading from among syndicated material, received daily, and his intimate knowledge of local customs easily compensated for his limited perspective. Moreover, being a native of the village and achieving success in a recognized employment gave him access to all levels of society, from the lowliest elements working on surrounding farms to the most exclusive social circles. The editor had a unique connection with the community, and his newspaper, read and discussed by every literate member of the community, was the only form of literature capable of shaping community cultural tastes.

If the accounts of realistic writers can be trusted, it seems, however, that few editors accepted for themselves, or as policy for their newspaper, the high purpose of broadening the cultural perspective of the community. Their purpose seems to have been much more practical: to ingratiate themselves into the goodwill of their middle class peers and to succeed at all costs in their business enterprise. The content of their publication was concerned mostly with "poking mild fun at the shams—the town pharisees," sending "nine or ten thousand people" weekly "to bed on this kind of mental pabulum."[4] As a result the small-town newspaper tended to insulate the small town people even further in their provincial ways and reinforce the middle class code of behavior—or middle class respectability.

William Allen White (*In Our Town*) says that the format he used for the Emporia *Gazette* was typical of hundreds of small town papers across the country. On the first page, "the parlor of the paper," the *Gazette* featured news of national and international significance with formal headings placed in bold type. The remainder of the daily newspaper, however, was devoted exclusively to local events. Beginning with the second page, says the editor: ". . . they and we go around in our shirt sleeves, calling people by their first names; teasing the boys and girls good-naturedly; tickling the pompous members of the village family with straws from time to time, and letting out the family secrets of the community without much regard for the feelings of the supercilious."[5]

Whereas White had drawn national attention by means of his commentary upon events of regional and national interest, reprinted from the *Gazette* in newspapers around the country, the financial success of his newspaper, as he well knew, depended upon his reputation among a few thousand subscribers in Emporia and the surrounding area. Therefore, to sell newspapers and thus insure future prosperity, White directed the news mostly to the general welfare of his region of Kansas and embellished the pages with intimacies of local inhabitants.

Like his counterpart in Emporia, the editor of the Winesburg *Eagle* in *Winesburg, Ohio* seems to have discovered the key to unlock the doors to material success. The omniscient narrator of Sherwood Anderson's "The Thinker" says:

> The paper on which George worked had one policy. It strove to mention by name in each issue, as many as possible of the inhabitants of the village. Like an excited dog, George Willard ran here and there, noting on his pad of paper who had gone on business to the county seat or had returned from a visit to a neighboring village. All day he wrote little facts upon the pad. "A. P. Wringlet had received a shipment of straw hats. Ed Byerbaum and Tom Marshall were in Cleveland Friday. Uncle Tom Sinnings is building a new barn on his place on the Valley Road."[6]

Using the newspaper as a means of ingratiation, giving the people what they wanted rather than what they needed to hear, seems to have been common practice among small town editors. The practice was so widespread that national agencies found it profitable to write circulating exchange items which, changed slightly, had wide application. During his apprenticeship under his father, the editor of the *Union of*

States, Ned Westlock in E. W. Howe's *The Story of a Country Town,* reports that these exchange articles containing general, laudatory descriptions of American village life frequently passed over the editor's desk and all the editor needed to do was to make minor adjustments in the content and substitute his town, Twin Mounds, for the name of the town in the article. The youthful apprentice questions the ethics of using such articles but finally defends the practice on the grounds that all newspapers used these items and that "it pleased the people who did not see the exchanges and who no doubt regarded it as a very real compliment."[7]

William Allen White defends this editorial practice by arguing that it helps prevent social cleavage from developing in the community. "Certainly by poking mild fun at the shams—the town pharisees—we make it difficult to maintain the class lines which the pretenders would establish."[9] He suggests that attempts to prevent the middle class citizens from taking themselves too seriously relax small-town stratification and help create a truly democratic society. But using the newspaper for this purpose would seem to have quite the opposite effect. Would not the very selection of prominent persons for notoriety in the local paper tend to make them seem more important to their neighbors and, by special recognition, feed the egos of those aspiring to social prominence? White's defense raises as many questions as it answers and still leaves serious doubts about the editorial policy— and social consciousness—of the small town editor.

While emphasis upon local events may have had some social purpose, as White suggests, other factors seem to have been more influential in helping to shape editorial policy. In some communities the newspaper was owned by other citizens or groups of citizens in the town, and in all towns the newspaper was dependent upon local sales. Whereas the office received a small income from printing handbills, notices, and stationery for individuals and merchants, the main source of revenue came directly from its local advertising and circulation.[9] The financial dependence of the paper upon its reputation in the town, therefore, guided its management to consider constantly the newspaper's public image in the community. The editor and his staff were thus sensitive to the unpopular and controversial, or to news not relevant to the local scene because adverse publicity in one way or another affected the paper's reputation and, ultimately, threatened all sources of income. In *The Story of a Country Town* Howe shows the uneasy relationship existing between the newspaper and its public and the tensions under which the editor labors. Following his father's disappearance, Ned Westlock had taken over the editorship of the *Union of States* in Twin Mounds. Immediately Ned comes to recognize the unique predicament the editor faces in attempting to please his audience. Ned complains that the village newspaper, unlike other local business enterprises, is constantly open to public inspection.

> Other trades and professions are more secret, and their contemptible transactions generously hid from the public, but all my work had to be submitted to the criticism of every idle vagrant who cared to pick up a sheet. . . . Public attention is always called to a newspaper, for otherwise it cannot prosper, and as the people are usually disgusted when they realize how little a man can do, papers of the class I published were not popular. Other men's affairs were equally contemptible, but they were charitably hid from the public gaze, whereas mine were regarded as common property, and fault found accordingly.[10]

Bound by this uneasy relationship with its clientele, there is little wonder that editors exercised restraint in forming editorial policy and that they adjusted the content to the interests and tastes of their uncultured audience.

Pragmatic reasons, nevertheless, were not the only influences shaping editorial policy. Making the newspaper a vehicle for carrying local information about the town and its people seems, for the most part, to have been an innocent procedure and, when applied with restraint and good judgment, doubtless gave the town necessary cohesiveness. As Dean Alfred Vivian of the College of Agriculture, Ohio State University, stated in 1921: "The home-town paper speaks not with an individual voice, but for the community, not to individuals but to everyone, from the rich man on the hill to the poor man in the roadside cottage. Nothing goes further toward unifying a neighborhood than a good weekly or semi-weekly."[11] Especially in the small country towns, local news about neighbors the townspeople saw only on Sundays and special occasions could serve to give the isolated farmers a certain sense of esprit de corps. The main fault with such editorial practices, however, seems to have been that the "mental pabulum" was out of proportion to its relative merit. In order to please their reading public, these newspapers deemphasized events of national and international significance and, in doing so, reinforced the notion already prevalent in most towns that the really important events of the world happen in the immediate vicinity.[12]

While it seems they played a key role in promoting and reinforcing provincial attitudes among the townspeople, few small town editors were singled out by realistic writers for special attention. In his severe censure of the middle class and their values in *Main Street*, Sinclair Lewis lists the editor of the Gopher Prairie *Weekly Dauntless* among those responsible for perpetuating the narrow attitudes of the town and, by extracting printed items from the newspaper, demonstrated the limited scope of news carried in the *Dauntless*. But Lewis does not expose the editor as an instrument of provinciality. Of the major realistic writers only William Dean Howells and Edgar Lee Masters drew attention to the corrupting influences of the small town editor, though neither author gave sufficient indication that his caricatures were characteristic of the profession.

In Howells's *A Modern Instance*, Bartley Hubbard revives the defunct Equity *Free Press* and makes it into a self-supporting operation. Hubbard is well suited for newspaper work in the small town; his lack of any fixed convictions enables him to meet each situation objectively and, at the same time, prevents his having any scruples about giving his subscribers exactly what he knows intuitively they want to read. The narrator says of his editorial practices: "He moulded the newspaper upon the modern conception, through which the country press must cease to have any influence in public affairs, and each paper became little more than an open letter of neighborhood gossip."[12] Hubbard takes a pragmatic approach to journalism: if his practices as editor meet with the approval of his respectable reading public, thus stimulating sales of his paper, they are then justified, even if these practices encourage the worst instincts in the village character. Hubbard's perceptiveness of small town mores in Equity brings success to the *Free Press* and elevates Hubbard to a position of respect in the community.

Though a young and eager opportunist, lacking character and personal conviction, Bartley Hubbard does not use his influence in the community for corruption. However, both editors in Edgar Lee Masters's collection of small town portraits, *Domesday Book* and *Spoon River Anthology*, deliberately distort the news media to gain personal respect and financial success. Editor Lowell of the *Times* in *Domesday Book* aborted the very purpose of his profession in his monomaniacal drive to become the voice of respectability in Leboy. Conscious of public opinion, Editor Lowell withholds from his readers the official position of the *Times* on controversial issues until he first determines the side most popular with his readers. Then he enters the conflict, throwing the weight and influence of his newspaper behind the popular side in an effort to unite the forces and bring the controversy to a speedy conclusion. For fear of adverse criticism, he plays down or suppresses entirely all sensational items, even when the situation demands wide exposure. Thus through crafty editing methods, Editor Lowell makes the *Times* a popular success in Leboy and builds a private fortune for himself.[14]

From his grave and thus protected from public exposure, Editor Wheden in *Spoon River Anthology* makes a full disclosure of his unethical business practices. He admits having deliberately chosen the most advantageous side in controversial issues in order to achieve his "cunning ends." Boastfully recalling his former power and influence, he demonstrates how with a few carefully chosen words he had been able to build or break reputations it had taken villagers a lifetime to build.

>   To be able to see every side of every question;
> To be on every side, to be everything, to be nothing long;
> To pervert truth, to ride it for a purpose,
> To use great feelings and passions of the human family
> For base designs, for cunning ends,
> To wear a mask like the Greek actors—
> Your eight-page paper—behind which you huddle,
> Bawling through the megaphone of big type;
> "This is I, the giant,"[15]

Ironically, at his death the town has interred Editor Wheden in a section of the graveyard containing an abundance of human waste and corruption, "where the sewage flows from the village, and empty cans and garbage are dumped, and abortions hidden."

While Editor Wheden is atypical of the treatment editors have received in studies of the small town, Masters's portrait does reveal an important insight into the interaction between the editor and his town. The editor held a powerful position of influence, and his newspaper, read and discussed by every literate member of the community, was the only form of written communication capable of shaping the social customs of the villagers. As Col. Wilkerson said in his address to the Missouri Association of Editors and Publishers in 1876, "If there is one power more potent than another for good, when under the proper influences; if there is one engine more powerful then any other for evil, when in bad hands, that power, that engine is the newspaper."[16] This influence could be used, as Editor Wheden shows, for personal gain or corruption. Or, this influence could help broaden the interests of the community, helping the people recognize their relationship not only to their neighbors but to the nation and world. It seems, however, from fear of risk or from the need for personal acceptance, most small town editors chose to shape the content of their newspaper to the demands of their reading public, making the newspaper a conveyer of local gossip, thus subverting their obligations as professional members of the press.[17]

Remarkably, realistic writers seldom singled them out as instruments of small town provincialism. In retrospect, their oversight seems all too obvious! Most of the realistic writers providing the evidence were either editors themselves or had risen to prominence from that profession. As William Cooper Howells, an ill-paid antislavery journalist, moved from town to town in the Midwest, the young William Dean Howells contributed his part to the family income by spending long hours setting type and writing local news items and poetry for his father's paper. Between the years 1856–1861 Howells, then only in his late teens and early twenties, served on the prestigious *Ohio State Journal* as reporter, exchange editor and editorial writer. Through his literary contributions to the *Journal* Howells attracted the national attention which started him on his way toward the editorships of the *Atlantic Monthly* and the *Harper's*

Monthly. Likewise, Edgar Watson Howe rose to prominence as a small town editor. Following the Civil War Howe's father purchased a newspaper operation in Bethany, Missouri, and at the age of eleven the youthful Howe began his apprenticeship in the printer's trade. After leaving Bethany, Howe worked as an itinerant printer and typesetter in several Midwestern towns before finally entering partnership in a newspaper in Golden, Colorado, at nineteen and assuming his first position as editor. In 1877 he and his older half-brother, James Howe, began the *Daily Globe* in Atchison, Kansas. In his thirty-six years as editor of the *Daily Globe,* Howe became known nationally as "the sage of Potato Hill, the philosopher of common sense."[18] William Allen White also held several positions on Midwestern newspapers as a young man, but unlike Howe and Howells, White had the benefits of a more extensive formal education. Just five years after leaving Kansas State University to assume the job as business manager of the El Dorado *Republican,* White bought the Emporia *Gazette,* the newspaper with which he built his national reputation.[19]

Among the realists, these writers have provided the most detailed studies of the small town editor. But it seems their sympathies, their nearness to the subject, or their realization of the complexities of running a business in the small town may well have blinded them to the role small town editors played as guardians of respectability.

NOTES

[1]The terms *small town* and *village* are used interchangeably in this paper.

[2]Everett Carter, *Howells and the Age of Realism* (New York: J. B. Lippincott, 1954), p. 103.

[3]Sinclair Lewis, *Main Street* (New York: Harcourt, Brace, 1920), p. 156.

[4]William Allen White, *In Our Town* (New York: McClure, Phillips, 1906), p. 6.

[5]White, p. 6.

[6]Sherwood Anderson, *Winesburg, Ohio* (1919; rpt. New York: Viking, 1966), p. 134.

[7]Edgar Watson Howe, *The Story of a Country Town* (1883; rpt. New York: Dodd, Mead, 1927), p. 185.

[8]White, p. 6.

[9]John Hicks, *Adventures of a Tramp Printer: 1880–1890* (Kansas City, Mo,: Midamerica Press, 1950), p. 17.

[10]Howe, pp. 264–65.

[11]Millard Van Marter Atwood, *The Country Newspaper* (Chicago: McClurg, 1923), p. 56.

[12]See Gerald K. Wells, "Caste and Code in the American Village," Diss. Univ. of South Carolina, 1972, p. 105.

[13]William Dean Howells, *A Modern Instance* (1882; rpt. Cambridge, Mass,: Riverside Press, 1923), p. 23.

[14]Edgar Lee Masters, *Domesday Book* (New York: MacMillan, 1920), pp. 103–04.

[15]Edgar Lee Masters, *Spoon River Anthology* (1915; rpt. New York: MacMillan, 1962), p. 134.

[16]*History and Transactions of the Editors and Publishers' Association of Missouri: 1867–1876* (Canton, Mo.: Canton Press Print, 1876), p. 9.

[17]See Atwood, p. 59.

[18]Gene A. Howe, "My Father was the most wretchedly unhappy man I ever knew," in *Post Biographies of Famous Journalists*, ed. John E. Drewry (Athens, Ga.: Univ. of Georgia Press, 1942), p. 187.

[19]See for biography of Howells and Howe, *Dictionary of American Biography*, ed. Harris E. Starr (New York: Charles Scribner's Sons, 1944), pp. 325–26; for White, *Twentieth Century Authors*, ed. Stanley J. Kunitz and Howard Haycroft (New York: H. W. Wilson Company, 1942), p. 1513.

Ellen Douglas's Small Towns:
Fictional Anchors

MICHAEL P. DEAN

In September 1979 Ellen Douglas published *The Rock Cried Out,* her fifth work of fiction, the most recent since the highly acclaimed *Apostles of Light* in 1973. The new work, a gripping narrative centered around events in Mississippi during the 1960s and early 1970s, reinforces previous estimates of her talent. Indeed, this latest novel has caused her fellow Greenvillian Shelby Foote to conclude, "What we see here, if we're watching, is the growth of a reputation; Ellen Douglas improves with every outing."[1] Since the appearance of her first novel in 1961, Ellen Douglas's fiction has slowly but steadily developed in scope, impact, and appeal to a growing number of dedicated readers. Her works—*A Family's Affairs* (1961); *Black Cloud, White Cloud* (1964); *Where the Dreams Cross* (1968); *Apostles of Light* (1973); and *The Rock Cried Out* (1979)—clearly establish her importance among contemporary American writers.[2]

In the fiction of Ellen Douglas many elements elicit praise, not the least of which are her skillful use and deeply-felt sense of setting or place. Her fictions are set in the mythic towns of Homochitto, located on the Mississippi River, and Phillippi, Mississippi, in the Delta. Clearly, the creation of Homochitto owes something to Natchez, while Phillippi's existence depends to some extent on Greenville. *The Rock Cried Out* is set in Chickasaw Ridge, Mississippi, a hamlet located in Homochitto County, several miles out in the country from Homochitto itself. Douglas's portrayal of all three towns as small is a function of both realism and the author's artistic design. A study of this portrayal reveals that Ellen Douglas uses small town settings to provide, paradoxically, both restriction and freedom, order and image, to her work.

Douglas's choice of settings is clearly not accidental. She chooses to place her work in small towns familiar to her because they offer a chance to observe the complexity of life in an intimate manner. The sprawl of large cities is disorienting. The chaos produced by such places creates flux, a constant shifting that defies the attempt to impose order. On the other hand, the suburbs produce homogeneity; they breed blandness. Their excessive regimentation is stultifying, deadening, ultimately lifeless. Thus Ellen Douglas turns to small towns because they provide a cross section of humanity on a scale that is easily grasped. Indeed, the diverse spectacle of human life the small town offers actively confronts and engages the observer. As Douglas has said, "The tensions are more immediate, the extremes of poverty more apparent—usually right under your nose. The whole network of people's lives becomes more apparent to you."[3] Rather than inhibiting her work, the use of small town settings frees it because it allows her to work with the materials she knows best. Within the small town setting "the whole network of people's lives" becomes clear in a way it never does either in an urban setting, where the complex network sprawls beyond the ordering power of the artist, or in a suburban one, where the network has loosened and frayed.

These materials she knows best (again, "the whole network of people's lives"), developed in the settings of small Mississippi towns, are not, however, restricted to such towns. They encompass the vast, intricate arrangement that we call human existence. Douglas herself has made precisely this point: "I'm not a sociologist. I write about the human condition. I have written about the place I know and the time I know, and how people live in that place and time . . . about the areas of human experience where I have observed the greatest stress."[4] As one would expect, then, her work deals with life and death, with love and hate, with the compromises people make with their neighbors—and with themselves.

Douglas's fiction is rooted in time and place, and this anchoring provides much strength for her work. Each of her books, however, increasingly manages to transcend the specificity of time and place in order to remind us of the universal stresses and demands of the human condition. Her fiction illustrates Dryden's phrase, "mankind is ever the same, and nothing lost out of Nature, though everything is altered."[5] Or to use the words of one of the characters in *The Rock Cried Out*, " 'Do you think there's someplace in the world that's different from here?' . . . I hadn't known I was going to say that, but saying it, I meant what I hadn't known" (p. 245).

Turning to the specific use Ellen Douglas makes of place in her fiction, one finds many functions of the small town settings. If we concentrate on three particular aspects of her social and physical settings, I think we will see the power that place gives her work. For convenience, we can label these aspects diversity, structures or buildings, and continuity.

To understand the apparent paradox of diversity in a small town we need only to return to Douglas's statement about her use of small town settings, in which she notes that the small town offers a writer the opportunity to work with the whole range of humanity on a scale that is sufficiently reduced to be grasped, to be ordered. The American small town is a microcosm of American humanity; for Ellen Douglas the microcosm is more intensely alive and usable than the macrocosm. The writer using a small town as setting resembles the resident of the small town; that is, they both know the inhabitants in an intimate way that is denied to those outside the confines of the town. Douglas expresses this idea early in *A Family's Affairs:* "Charlotte had known him all her life with the intimate, impersonal small-town knowledge that begins at children's parties and grows with the marriages and deaths of mutual cousins" (p. 4). And such intimate knowledge is not restricted to one segment of small town society, for Ellen Douglas fills her novels with a broad range of characters, from a derelict, down-on-his-luck guitar player to "a lady who claims descent from Charlemagne by way of Robert the Bruce" and shares, consequently, "a collateral connection" with Mary, Queen of Scots (*Where the Dreams Cross*, p. 3). But Douglas's novels are not given over to either eccentrics or stereotypes; instead, she populates her small towns with the real people one would expect to find there: good and evil, rich and poor, black and white, kind and cruel—but human, all of them very human.

Diversity in Ellen Douglas's small towns is not confined to population alone. Variety in scene, another kind of diversity, is clearly depicted in the story "Jesse" from *Black Cloud, White Cloud.* "Very few of Phillippi's respectable Negroes live on Pearl Street, particularly if they have children. It's a noisy neighborhood, the red-light houses sandwiched in between nightclubs like the Casablanca and the Live and Let Live; tumbledown fish markets, Chinese grocery stores, cafés and secondhand clothing and furniture stores crowded into a ten-block slum. But it was the right neighborhood for an old-time jazz musician, and I thought nothing of Jesse's living there" (p. 95). In this passage we see the natural diversity of the small town. When the narrator says, "I thought nothing of Jesse's living there," she does not mean that she is insensitive or indifferent to Jesse, rather, that Jesse and his life (and the life of those around him) are a part of the human condition. This "noisy neighborhood" is a part of Phillippi, and its residents are citizens of Phillippi. The narrator of this story, like Ellen Douglas herself, is wise enough to know that such a neighborhood should not be denounced or ignored. Instead, it must be accepted for what it is, part of Phillippi, part of the order of life that Phillippi presents. And when accepted as part of this order, it can be placed and dealt with on the terms it demands and needs—its own.

One further dimension of diversity deserves comment: the richness of small town life. This aspect is well illustrated in a description of Homochitto in *A Family's Affairs.* "The sisters from the Catholic orphanage in dark blue, full-skirted habits, their winged white hats standing out stiff and dazzling in the summer sunshine, marched the orphans home from Mass. The Cathedral bell struck every hour. Horses's hoofs clopped on the still morning streets, and the vegetable man called out his long-drawn chant. . . . Homochitto invented itself in Anna's mind so lavishly she knew a whole summer would not be long enough to take in all its life" (p. 106).

These observations are placed in the mind of young Anna McGovern, but the point of the passage is applicable to more than one child and one summer. The small towns in the work of Ellen Douglas teem with life, and a whole summer, indeed a whole lifetime, is not enough to take it all in.

We may say, then, that diversity is one element of small town existence that draws Ellen Douglas's attention. Diversity in the small town reflects order because it allows complexity to be dealt with in a comprehensible, understandable way; it reflects image because it reveals clearly the whole network of people's lives, a network that finally has a universal scale.

The connection between structures and Douglas's use of small town settings is easier to discern, I think, than the notion of diversity in small town settings. Towns are composed of people and buildings; the two ingredients are required if a writer wishes to avoid depicting nomads or ghost towns. But in Douglas's fiction, structures, particularly houses and churches, take on a significance that expands far beyond their normal roles as shelters. Indeed, the lives of these small town inhabitants are so bound up in buildings that the latter seem to take on a life of their own, as if they existed not simply to serve their occupants but were in some unfathomable way alive.

In all of Ellen Douglas's novels structures dominate, regulate, and reflect the lives of the characters who build, use, and inhabit them. In *A Family's Affairs* much space is given over to the Anderson and McGovern homes in Homochitto. The very title of the novella "The House on the Bluff" (from *Black Cloud, White Cloud*) reveals its concern with a human habitation. *Where the Dreams Cross* is concerned not only with the Hunter family's modest cottage in Phillippi but also with a commissary, a cotton gin, a formerly magnificent courthouse, a burned-down plantation house, and the Mid-South Hardware Store, "the oldest continuously operated hardware store in the state of Mississippi." (p. 218). *Apostles of Light* is dominated by the Clarke-Griswold house, a structure that comes to seem so much alive that we understand a character's setting it afire; he wants to destroy it in the same way one might wish to destroy an evil man. Finally, *The Rock Cried Out,* though set in the hamlet of Chickasaw Ridge, gives us a number of structures, including an old family home, a cabin that the narrator of the novel rebuilds, or better, restructures (as he attempts to restructure his life), and a SPASURSTA, a Naval Space Surveillance Station that projects us forward into the next century just as the "big house" at Chickasaw Ridge carries us back into the last.

A few examples from this multitude will serve as illustrations of Douglas's use of structures. In *A Family's Affairs* the Anderson family home in Homochitto is revealed through the impression it makes on young Anna McGovern:

> The house sat close to the street behind a wrought-iron fence, crowded on one side against a dark red brick, turreted house of the 1870's with a round tower like Rapunzel's prison, a steep, gray slate roof, and windows with leaded panes of colored glass; on the other side, its yard stretched away to an adjoining three-story mansion of the nineties with jigsaw trim and an octagonal sun parlor; across the street were the cathedral and the park. . . . At the back, invisible from the street, two-story brick wings faced each other across a brick-paved court, joined to the house by a covered walkway from the latticed back porch to the old outdoor kitchen in the west wing. And quite hidden away behind the east wing was a tiny brick building that had been her great-grandfather's office and was now the children's playhouse. . . . There was nothing she could add to it in imagination, nothing she could edit away, no way she could make it more or less than itself. . . . This house was so full of its own life, so specific and so vigorous in its impact upon hers, that the act of taking it in used her whole attention. It was the most formidable, the most interesting, the strangest, the most familiar and commonplace, the most *exciting* house in the world. . . .
>
> Here was the parlor with every piece of furniture exactly where it had been last summer, the rug worn in the same places, the same dust on the gold and maroon Empire urns, the splintery floor still marked with a dark stain where little Ralph had spilled a bowl of mayonnaise. Here, in this shabby house, lived in not with apology but with pride, was the mysterious emotion that was the keystone of her family's life. Here, more than anywhere else, it was clear that there was an instantly recognizable way in which real people acted. . . .
>
> Like those primitive people to whom the name of the tribe is the word for The Men, Anna called the limits of her life by a larger name, and joyfully claimed that this prison built of love and pride was the universe. (pp. 106–09)

We can see that the house assumes a role of its own, as if it in some way becomes a town within a town and its furniture plays the role of structures within structures. This specification of furniture is not haphazard. Later in the novel furniture is used a number of times to reflect character, to project order and image. The concern with furniture as an integral part of structures (as structures themselves are an integral part of towns) runs throughout Douglas's work. For example, *The Rock Cried Out* concludes with the narrator's sitting at his work table, a table made by him of cherry cut in his own woods and assembled with the screws on the bottom rather than the top, an improvement over Uncle D's from an earlier generation (p. 300).

The use of church buildings in Ellen Douglas's fiction deserves special notice. Churches, like school houses and old family homes, are important structures in small towns. As we might expect, they play important roles in Douglas's writings. The following passage in *A Family's Affairs* shows not only the importance of churches to the order and image of small towns, but the author's ability to imbue inanimate structures with a sense of animation.

> There are places, buildings, everywhere, that are so strongly associated with the lives of certain people that they seem to those who love or hate them to possess a brooding, immobile life of their own; and this was true of the Presbyterian Church in Homochitto. Every one of all Kate's family gathering for her funeral had felt, clearly or obscurely, at one time or another, that that square, spare, sturdy, beautiful building *lived*, that somehow the molecules crystallized in its walls of brick and plaster were the same molecules that flowed in their own frail, impermanent veins. It didn't matter that the notion was a silly and unreasonable one. They had all felt it, had cherished the feeling, and had longed on occasion to express it. (p. 430)

As we might expect, churches play similar roles in other novels. In *Apostles of Light* the destruction of an early nineteenth-century Methodist church symbolizes the deterioration of human sensitivity and feeling in twentieth-century Homochitto. In *The Rock Cried Out* the burning of Mercy Seat Church in the tumultuous summer of 1964 coincides with the senseless murder of a teenaged girl by a young boy unable to cope with feelings he can not even formulate. Private acts, the boy's inner seething, are duplicated by public ones, the church's material destruction.

Ellen Douglas's interest in using structures, particularly old family homes and churches, is another reason she uses small town settings. The tendency of small towns to change slowly and cautiously in appearance provides her with stable, slowly changing buildings. Hence, the Presbyterian church in Homochitto appears to be a solid rock in an ever-rushing tide of change: "A hundred and fifty years had passed since the church had been built in a new, raw land by settlers long rooted in an austere faith. A hundred and fifty years—not the full span of two lives as long as Kate's. But already the land, and the symbols so lovingly and so solidly constructed by the sojourners there, were old, an anachronism in a bewildering world, clung to tenaciously by men and women who could find nothing else so solid in the whirlwind of their lives" (p. 430). Houses take on an added sense of protectiveness when the town is viewed, as Homochitto is in "The House on the Bluff" in *Black Cloud, White Cloud,* as little more than a "temporary bastion against the surrounding wilderness" (p. 15). Seen in this way, structures—necessary elements of small towns—assume a role in Douglas's fiction that emphasizes the dependence of her writing on small town settings. James McGovern's plea to his son Ralph in *A Family's Affairs* looms large: "Whatever you do, whatever happens, don't sell the place" (p. 76). The loss of the house would mean the simultaneous end of order and image, the unleashing of chaos.

A third aspect of Douglas's small town settings, which I have designated continuity, is closely related to her use of structures. Structures provide a physical continuity through the ongoing presence of buildings. But what I mean by continuity involves spiritual continuity rather than physical continuity. Structures are tangible evidence of the linkage of generations, but the intangible linkage is accomplished through language, through the stories that connect the present with the past and, as time moves on and the present becomes past, with the future. Perhaps this point can be illustrated with F. Scott Fitzgerald's well-known description in *The Great Gatsby* of the trip north from Chicago to Minneapolis. There Nick Carraway describes himself as "a little solemn . . . a little complacent from growing up in the Carraway house in a city where dwellings are still called through the decades by a family's name."[6] The house itself provides the physical evidence of continuity, but the naming of the family, whether Carraway or Anderson or McGovern, provides the intangible evidence that reminds us of generations stretching back in time.

This interest in the continuity of generations is found in all of Ellen Douglas's novels. In *A Family's Affairs* we read of the first McGovern to reach Homochitto; he arrives on a flatboat at the end of the eighteenth century and settles down. His decendents can be found populating twentieth century Homochitto. And those descendents do look

back in an attempt to establish continuity. Anna McGovern says, "I'm
. . . interested. . . . I've been interested in all those old dead people
ever since Gran first told me the story about Henry Dupré drinking
the barrel of whisky in the cellar" (p. 329). The encroachment of
discontinuity, of disintegration of generations, is directly linked to the
abandonment of small towns and settlements and the ordering of
human life they provide. "Used to be," says a character in *Where the
Dreams Cross:* "Used to be, . . . and not so many years ago either,
you'd find all the men of the neighborhood, any afternoon you were
looking for them, gathered around the table in the back of the commissary. . . . But now! Half the time they're gone. They're throwing their
money away on the horses in Hot Springs. Or they're in Memphis or
New Orleans or New York City. . . . I don't like it. . . . I liked the olden
days. . . . Tradition! Continuity! That's what gives a man's life dignity"
(pp. 218–19).

In *Apostles of Light* the abandonment of aging Martha Clarke by
her nephews, and particularly by her grand-nephew, symbolizes the
abandonment of the generation of the past by the generation of the
present. George Clarke, a member of the generation caught in the
middle, articulates the discontinuity; "It seems to me, . . . we could
have just stuck with Aunt Martha" (p. 128). After being assured by his
son that Aunt Martha is happy at Golden Age Acres, he adds: "I think
about how the place used to be. . . . Always a house full of children.
And that summer we had the hawk. . . . I think about *myself*, too. . . .
Will it be like that for me when I'm old? When other people will be
making decisions for me? I tell you the truth, son, it'd be better for us
all if we'd done this the old way—like families used to do, when
everybody lived together and made the best of it. . . ." (p. 129). Later,
when George discusses the same concerns with his cousin Mary
Hartwell, Douglas writes that "there was an elegiac quality to their
conversation. They talked of old days. . . . Times gone, their very
quality irretrievable in this strange, cold, threatening world they and
their children lived in" (p. 263).

This conversation takes place in a Homochitto that has an express-
way and a Golden Ages Acres, a Homochitto that may be on the verge
of changing from the Homochitto of the earlier fiction. Indeed, this

sense of approaching change in Homochitto seems to account for the introduction of Chickasaw Ridge in the most recent novel. Ellen Douglas seems compelled to seek order and image in small towns, and so it is not surprising to find the narrator of *The Rock Cried Out,* Alan McLaurin, deeply attached to the hamlet of Chickasaw Ridge. His description of the family of his girlfriend Miriam reveals much about his (and Ellen Douglas's) need for the generational continuity of the small town.

> Her family seems to me to be cut loose from all that I grew up thinking of as natural. They live an uprooted life in one college town after another, moving up and down and sideways in the academic world. . . . But I doubt they've ever had a cousin on the Board of Supervisors, or had to find out who you persuade to dump a load of gravel on your road, or been personally acquainted with a sheriff's deputy. Such a phenomenon as a place in the United States to which a real American citizen is attached, which holds his past and considerable of the past of his parents and grandparents, and even his great-grandparents, the landscape of his nightmares and of all those dreams so sweet they make your teeth ache—the existence of such a place was unimaginable to Miriam until she began to know me. (p. 126–27)

Later, in a speech reminiscent of Anna McGovern's, he remarks, "I wanted to talk about old times with people like Noah," who is an eighty-five-year-old black patriarch (p. 144). The generational continuity sought by Alan and Anna can best be found in a Chickasaw Ridge or a Homochitto that maintains the form of a recognizable small town.

Small towns are the bedrock of Ellen Douglas's fiction. They anchor her writing firmly in time and place. They give, through her concentration on diversity, structures, and continuity, order to her work. In addition, they provide image to her fiction by giving her the ability to transcend the specificity of time and place to deal with the American experience and, ultimately, the universal stresses and demands, and triumphs and joys, of the human condition. Thus, Ellen Douglas uses the order and image of the small town in America as a technique for exploring life beyond the confines such a setting seems to imply. She knows the power small town settings can provide, and her knowledge places her work in a tradition that is shared by all those who record the passing American—and human—scene. This is an arduous and noble calling, and Ellen Douglas answers it well.

Michael P. Dean   171

NOTES

[1]Foote's remark is printed on the dust jacket of *The Rock Cried Out*.

[2]The first four books were published by Houghton Mifflin (Boston); the most recent is published by Harcourt Brace Jovanovich (New York). References to these works appear in the text.

[3]Billy Skelton, "G'ville Author Ellen Douglas Writes, Reads Consistently," *Clarion Ledger-Jackson Daily News*, 20 April 1969, Sec. A., p. 3.

[4]Mary Jayne Whittington, "Ellen Douglas: An Apostle of Light," *Jackson Magazine*, June 1978, p. 19.

[5]John Dryden, "Preface to the Fables," in *Essays of John Dryden*, ed. W. P. Ker (New York: Russell & Russell, 1961), II, 263.

[6]F. Scott Fitzgerald, *The Great Gatsby* (1925; rpt. New York: Scribners, 1953), p. 155.

Shelby Foote's Bristol in "Child by Fever"

ROBERT L. PHILLIPS

According to Eudora Welty time and place are the raw ingredients of fiction. Hers is a typically Southern point of view. Time as history, the past, and place as community, typically the small town, are common to much Southern fiction, and they are the material from which Shelby Foote has constructed his five novels and the stories collected in a book, *Jordan County*. Place for Foote is most often the Mississippi Delta; three novels, *Tournament* (1949), *Love in a Dry Season* (1951), *Follow Me Down* (1950), and the stories in *Jordan County* (1954), are set in Foote's fictional Delta county. In two novels, *Shiloh* (1952) and the recent novel, *September, September*, Foote leaves Jordan County, but both books have characters who are natives of the county and its principal town, Bristol.

Jordan County and the town of Bristol resemble in both geography and history Foote's native county, Washington County, and his home town, Greenville. Foote admits that "the geography is the same," and it takes only a casual glance at the history of the region to find significant parallels between the "real" and the "fictional." *Tournament* is about a figure, Hugh Bart, who is very much like Foote's grandfather, Huger (Hugh) Foote. The history of the Wingate-Sturgis family in "Child by Fever," the long central story in *Jordan County*, resembles that of the Blanton-Theobold family which gave the land for New Greenville; (Old Greenville was burned by Yankees and what remained washed into the Mississippi River.)

In using history, as he does, Foote follows the worn path Faulkner, Warren, and many other Southern writers have followed, and he is traveling in the company of his fellow Greenvillian, Walker Percy. In

172

writing on Percy, the historian Edward Cashin, has discussed what
these Southern novelists have accomplished in their use of history:

> There is an indeterminate but very real point when a people's history
> becomes internalized. Myth becomes mores. When that happens to a tribe
> or a nation, then the history as understood becomes more true than the
> history which historians seek to define. The novelist is a better historian of
> history-as-mores than the professional writer of history-as-it-happened.
> The novelist reaches deep into his pscyhe for his history, and he communi-
> cates readily to a wide audience because his readers recognize the same
> attitudes and perceptions within themselves.[1]

When Foote turns to a fictional examination of the town Bristol he
casts that examination in terms of historical process. The conclusions
his examination reveal are the familiar modernist conclusions that
twentieth-century man inhabits a wasteland of his own making. The
uniquenesses in Foote lie in the particular geography and history that
he knows, that of the Mississippi Delta, and in his concern for the
community, for Bristol, and for the fates of individual citizens. In
contrast to much serious twentieth-century modernist fiction which,
following the practices of psychological realism, delves exclusively
into the psyches of failed human beings, Foote's treatment of Bristol as
not simply a physical place but a body of men with communal needs
and ambitions gives his town a major dramatic role in his story.

Foote's modern Bristol is the synthesis of a dialectical process
which pits an artificial agrarian ideal against a bourgeois middle class;
it is a synthesis which does not result from the strengths of either of the
antitheses, however, but rather from the weaknesses and failures of
both. Bristol, born of the failure of the agrarian ideal and the inability
of the middle class to come to terms with itself, has failed. Foote finds
no cultural forces operating which give the town coherent civic purpose, no sense of adhering faithfully to a cultural pattern of fulfilling a
historical destiny. During the first decades of the twentieth century
the town has an ambivalent uneasiness about its past. It has no idea of
what it wants to become, and it is decidedly unhappy with what it is.

"Child by Fever,"[2] the central novelette in *Jordan County*, provides
one of Foote's clearest statements about the history of the Mississippi
Delta and the role of the town as a character in history. In "Child by
Fever" he treats the decline of the agrarian ideal and the inability of

middle-class Bristol to use its own inherent strengths which could provide an ethos to replace the lost source of collective regional security.

Hector Sturgis is Foote's heir of the short-lived and superficial agrarian ideal. By inheritance Hector was a member of the landed gentry that in the antebellum agrarian society provided social, political, and economic leadership for many parts of the South. If one was to be a leader, one had to have not only requisite possessions but a close relationship with the community. In his biography of Stonewall Jackson, Allen Tate described the relationship between the agrarian aristocrat and his community:

> Without possessions a man did not morally exist. The idea of the "inner life," held by the Calvinist people in far-off New England, had no meaning. In the South, the man as he appeared in public was the man: his public appearance was his moral life. The nearest equivalent to the "inner life" was "private affairs." The New Englander was mystical, religious; the Southerner, practical, materialistic. Private affairs were not enquired into and they had no public value. A man's property was his character.[3]

The agrarian achieved his position through a relationship with the community. The agrarian, to be a man and a leader, had a public role to play.

Hector's downfall actually began before his time; it began with his grandfather. His great grandfather, the first Hector Wingate, had come to Jordan County in 1835, one of the first settlers. This Hector subdued a large tract of Jordan County jungle and completed just months before his death in the Mexican War, in 1845, the large plantation house which was the visible symbol of his public character. The second Hector Wingate inherited land and house in 1845, but by not assuming the role of military leadership in the Civil War sixteen years later, he failed to live up to his own and the county's expectations. This Hector "felt that he had failed his heritage," and after the defeat he "turned bitter" (pp. 78–79). In bitterness he began to neglect the wife he had married in 1858, and the daughter born in 1860, so that Mrs. Wingate turned to her daughter, Esther, for the attention her husband did not provide. Esther endured her mother's affection for eighteen years. Then, on Christmas Eve, 1877, just two months after her embittered father "was killed by a negro tenant following a disagreement over settlement for the '77 crop" (p. 84), Esther announced to her mother that she had to marry the Irish tenor in the Episcopal church choir whom she had managed to seduce. Esther married John Sturgis in March and in September Hector was born.

Mrs. Wingate had to surrender to inevitable defeat at the hands of her daughter. At the wedding she bore herself "like a general at a surrender following a battle lost to guile and superior numbers" (p. 89). The grandson, however, would be hers. Hector Sturgis's mother had little to say about her son's upbringing, and his father had nothing to say at all. For the first fifteen years of his life, from 1878 until 1893, when Mrs. Wingate died of yellow fever, the grandmother dominated the boy.

Mrs. Wingate made Hector into an effeminate monster unfit for a public or private role, even though she thought she was preparing him for the highborn state to which his property entitled him. She did not dress him like other children. Hector wore "tight serge knee-breeches," "hightop button shoes and ribbed black stockings" and a "wide satin bow tie that rode up under his chin" (p. 99). On a typical occasion Mrs. Wingate refused Hector the wiener and lady finger the butcher and baker offered him when he went shopping with her. "How do we know what they use to stuff those things? Wait till we get home where we grind our own" (p. 101), she said of the wiener. "Don't you know they make those things with the leavings?" (p. 101), she said of the baker's lady finger. Naturally butcher and baker regard her with "cold hostility," but Hector realizes that "they were afraid of her" and "it made him proud that she was his grandmother" (p. 101).

Having found public school unacceptable for Hector, Mrs. Wingate had him tutored at home. She then sent him to a "boarding school in Virginia." Hector's acceptance among his classmates came more from their impressions of Mrs. Wingate than from their admiration for Hector. In 1892, two of the boys spent Christmas holidays with Hector; the boys described the Wingate plantation as "something out of the Middle Ages" and Mrs. Wingate as "a lady of the old school" (p. 120).

A year and a half after the boy's visit, Mrs. Wingate died of yellow fever. When Hector finally was allowed to return home, he discovered that his mother had not only assumed Mrs. Wingate's role but had tried to assimilate as nearly as possible Mrs. Wingate's personality. "As soon as she was able to sit up in bed she began to wear the dead woman's clothes; she even held her mouth awry, irked and bitter-looking . . ." (p. 124). Hector was no more able to rebel against Esther Sturgis than he had been able to rebel against Mrs. Wingate. He simply had no interest in independence and so he too failed his heritage. A twenty-Negro clause (exempting those who owned twenty slaves or more) in the Confederate Conscription Act had excused his grandfather from the Civil War, but in 1898 Esther Sturgis simply would not allow the third Hector to march off to the Spanish-American War. When Hector tried to join Captain Barcroft's Bristol volunteers, telling his mother that he would be sworn in, she simply said "I reckon not" and rested her unchallenged case on the value of Hector's "fifteen thousand dollar education" (p. 126).

Marriage had been an act of defiance for Esther Sturgis, but when Hector eloped with Ella Lowery he brought his bride-of-an-hour to the Wingate-Sturgis mansion to introduce her to his mother. In marriage, as in everything else, Hector failed. He could not admit to himself that Homo sapiens is a mortal animal, heir to the pains and pleasures of animalhood. Fear of strange animals was one of his childhood traumas, and as a young adult the horror of the three-day labor attendant upon Ella's giving birth to an eighteen-pound fourth Hector made him forever incapable of playing the sexual role of husband. When the child died six months later, ending the Wingate-Sturgis line, Ella "recovered from both the birth and death of her child, . . . turned to Hector with the old urgency . . . and found no resurrection of the flesh" (pp. 154–55). Hector had peered through the bedroom door at Ella in labor six months before; the memory was a "reproach" to him "for having been the cause of all her suffering" (p. 155). Ella gave him six months, then returned to the life of promiscuity she had enjoyed before she married Hector. In the winter of 1910 they found her dead in the Bristol hotel, the victim of an apparent accident. The gas fumes also killed the salesman who had rented the room and who was wearing candy-striped shorts.

After Ella's death Hector retreated into the final isolation of insanity. He imagined that Ella's ghost had returned to him. The Sturgis servants told tales of what happened in his room, of his talking to himself and doing strange things. Neighbors told tales of the strange behavior they observed: his talking to animals on the road and his going to the woods to feed the birds. The attic of the Sturgis mansion had been his escape in early childhood; it was his private play-time kingdom, the only world he could command. From one of the rafters in the attic, in 1911, Hector Sturgis, at the insistence of Ella's ghost, hanged himself.

Hector was an utter failure as the agrarian aristocrat and as a human being, although his mother and grandmother had tried to shape him for a public role. After he had failed at public shool. Mrs. Wingate lectured him about his position.

> "Now listen," she said. . . . "There are really only two classes of people in this world, those who have and those who wish they had. . . . When those of the second class begin to realize that they will never catch up with those of the first, they jeer. . . . Those of the first class (which includes you . . .) must realize that the jeering goes with the having. Besides, when you are older and able to strike back at them, by foreclosing their mortgages or causing them to be dismissed from their places of employment, they will not jeer where you can hear them. . . . And what is said behind your back cannot matter, first because you cannot hear it and second because it is a sort of underhanded compliment in the first place. It's a certain sign that they acknowledge your position, a proof of membership. You understand?"
> "Yessum," he said, responding to another shake. But he did not. (p. 116)

When he returned home from the University of Virginia his mother tried to make a gentleman farmer out of him, but he was neither interested nor able. Finally Esther tried to make him into a kind of patriarch of Bristol. The town had grown rapidly during the 1880s and '90s, and Mrs. Sturgis, who was to become known as the "mother of Bristol," began to subdivide and develop her Wingate inheritance. Hector had always been interested in mechanical drawing, and Mrs. Sturgis decided that his talent might be useful to her real-estate projects. Hector's maps, according to Mr. Clinkscales, the Episcopalian rector, were the groundwork for "an Athens of the South" (p. 145). Hector enthusiastically threw himself into his work, and as his insanity grew upon him his drawings grew more particularized. In his last years Hector "began to add colors, green for trees and lawns, blue for water in drainage ditches and artificial ponds, red for underground installations, mains and sewers. By then black was reserved for details such as carriage blocks and arc lights, streetcars and delivery wagons, and finally the people themselves, as seen from above, going about their work and their pleasures. . . . at last the sheets resembled a futuristic painting, a bird's-eye view of Utopia, one to one hundred" (pp. 146–147). Later Mrs. Sturgis had the sheets "bound in tooled morocco" and presented them to the mayor who arranged for them to be displayed under glass in the courthouse. They stayed there twenty years—"the crowded, multi-colored sheets that had begun as maps and wound up resembling work done by a latter-day amateur Bruegel or Bosch looking down from a seat on the clouds" (p. 147). After Mrs. Sturgis's death the drawings were removed to the belfry. In the early 1950s an art critic from Memphis wrote a column in the *Commercial Appeal*. "He called his column 'The Last Romantic' and spoke of Hector Sturgis as an undiscovered genius" (p. 223). But Hector was no undiscovered genius; he was not equipped to be anything and in a society where one's public self *is* one's self the failure is fundamental. If Mrs. Sturgis was the "mother of Bristol," as the Bristol newspaper for years greeted her on her birthdays, then modern Bristol was the child of incest and failure, for Mrs. Sturgis insisted that Hector's drawings be carefully followed in developing East Bristol.

Foote devotes considerable attention to the people who inhabited Hector's Utopia and who did not find their situation as idyllic as Hector drew it. The narrative voice in the story often repeats what "people were saying" so that the community of Bristol, the collective view, becomes a major dramatic force in the story. The method Foote uses is reminiscent of Southern local color fiction of the last quarter of the nineteenth century and the first decades of the twentieth. Foote's narrator in "Child by Fever" is not as close to Bristol as Joel Chandler Harris's narrator was to Shady Dale; he is not as distant as Twain's narrator was from Hadleyburg, but he shares with both Harris and Twain a deep concern for his community. Harris's narrator often reported what "everybody said," happily including himself in the "everybody." He was satisfied to be one of the number in Shady Dale and agreed with the town's opinions. In "The Man That Corrupted

Hadleyburg," the narrator's pleasure was increased by his not being a member of the leading nineteen. Twain's narrator found Hadleyburg narrow, greedy, and vicious; he wanted no part of it. Foote's narrator treats Bristol in the third person plural; Bristol is always "they," not "we." The distance allows the narrator to comment and judge, but the town's views and reactions to the highborn Wingates and Sturgises are far more important to the narrator than they ever are to Hector himself.

Bristol had many of the same shortcomings as Twain's Hadleyburg, Sinclair Lewis's Gopher Prairie, or E. A. Robinson's Tilbury Town. The town could be narrow and hypocritical. Ella's promiscuity was certainly scandalous; the Baptist women, after all, had warned Ella's mother that some dire event lay in Ella's crooked path. But in judging Hector Sturgis, Bristol was neither judging him as a private citizen; nor was it limiting his freedom by imposing unnatural restraints. Hector was highborn; his designated role was a public one. The character of its agrarian leader was the property of Bristol, and if Bristol were to have passed into the twentieth century with its agrarian ideal unimpaired, Hector's position would have given the town the security of a social order defended by a Civil War and sanctioned in the historical romance which Hector had read. That was the public folkway, and a public interest in Hector was the natural outcome. "Not many people nowadays ever heard of [Hector Sturgis]," the narrator explains at the beginning of the tale. "Even fewer ever saw him, and no one at all ever knew him. But there were those who claimed to know his story, know it so well, they said, that between the time when Mrs. Sturgis died and six months later, when the house was razed, they could take you into the attic and point out the rafter beneath which he had brought it to a close: or so they claimed" (pp. 76–77).

Hector's failure reveals a conflict between Bristol's need for leadership and its refusal to accept the unworthy but natural heir to the role. The town's ambivalence was apparent in its reception of him in 1898 on his return from Charlottesville. "Those who stood on street corners in Bristol that summer after his graduation and saw him drive past—always in a hurry but going no place, an outlander, rakish and modern . . . watched him with amusement and even admiration, but with hardly any envy. They sniggered as he drove past. They nudged each other. They said, 'It's that Sturgis boy, home from college, a dude. I bet you he's hell with the ladies' " (p. 172). By one set of standards they condemn Hector, but being "hell with the ladies" was something Bristol could admire.

The town's response to Ella's death was a clear sign of its rejection of the court of Sturgis-Wingate and of its heir. As might be expected, her death was the talk of the town, but only the family, the minister and the undertaker dared to attend the funeral. Others rode by and looked.

> It was Ella—and, by inference, the Sturgis family with her—who held the limelight. . . . "If thats blue-blood," the night clerk had said, "I'm glad I didn't have any to pass on to my kids. If a man wants his wife to stay home, he by God ought to nail her down. You see what I mean?" For thirty-six hours the talk had been of little else—where she had been, whom she had been seen with, her partiality for traveling men—and when the thirty-six hours were up, they formed a parade out past the cemetery, just short of the lip of the grave." (p. 182)

Had Bristol looked to its own strengths it might have shaped public standards more workable and appropriate to a town than those of the agrarian order. There were three innate strengths which middle-class Bristol might have developed. The first strength was a basic regard for life and, growing out of that, was the second—vigorous sexuality. The third strength was its middle-class heritage to which in its own interests it should have been stubbornly loyal.

Bristol's basic regard for life appeared in its gossip about Ella's death. They condemned her on narrow, conventional grounds, but ringing through their talk was the realization that her death was a waste.

> People . . . passed [the news of Ella's death] along with an air of having foretold it. Women discussed it in grocery stores and over backyard fences. . . . "Have you heard about Ella Sturgis" Did you *ever?*" Men gathered on street corners and reviewed her life over bars and café counters, philosophizing on mortality and the sanctity of marriage . . . in defense and condemnation, alternately saturnine and sardonic. This death seemed such a waste. "They say you cant take it with you. Ha. By golly, she took it with her." (pp. 178–179)

The community condemned Ella's violations of its sexual taboos, but it was very much aware of its hypocrisy, for it had more than a secret admiration for her innocent and vigorous prostitution. Until she

married Hector and allied herself with the weakness of the Wingates
and Sturgises, she was potentially a figure upon whom Bristol could
redeem itself, for she had no regard for narrow standards of judgment.
She was somewhat like Herman Melville's Billy Budd at the fiddler's
green; she could participate in the petty vices of man and retain her
innocence. She simply refused to consider what she was doing to be
wrong and would not let contrary views interfere with her pleasure.
As a young lady,

> ... her only concern had been young men and thus she had acquired a
> reputation. When she was fourteen the watchers downtown would see her
> pass the barber shop or pool hall window, legs wobbly on high heels and
> wearing the flimsy, violent-flowered dresses she persuaded her mother to
> make for her—and returning, out of the tail of her eye, the stares of all the
> watchers. She not only seemed not to care what they thought, she seemed to
> go out of her way to make sure they understood that she did not care: so that,
> in the end, she showed how much she did care after all (but in reverse) and
> they responded with the frank, lickerish stares and the gossip she not only
> provoked but invited; it was reciprocal. (p. 136)

It was indeed reciprocal. The men of the town envied the drummer in
the striped shorts. They wished they could "go that way," if they had to
go at all. Ella was a mother-earth figure who missed her calling. After
her marriage she had to content herself with traveling salesmen; she
was prevented from performing her vital services for Bristol.

The character of John Sturgis represents Bristol's third basic
strength—its middle-class, bourgeois ethos. Before Esther Wingate
seduced him, Sturgis, the son of Barney Sturgis, an Irish barkeeper,
was on his way to becoming a substantial figure in Bristol—the sort of a
fellow a town could admire and its sons could emulate.

> Finishing high school he went to work for one of his father's customers. ...
> The boy did well, first in the [feed and grain merchant's] warehouse and
> then on the road. He was liked and even admired, and now in his middle
> twenties after six years in the business world he was being pointed to as a
> man on the way to success, an example of what could be done in that world
> by a young man who would apply himself, keep cheerful, and not grouse
> about salary or overtime. (p. 86)

The community approved of him, but John Sturgis failed the middle-
class ideal and whatever virtues it may have had. In the Wingate
mansion, where he had a room on the second floor, he listened to Mrs.

Wingate's condescending views about the Irish without so much as a whimper of protest. It is no surprise that his son could not later even remember what he looked like.

Bristol entered the twentieth century guided more by its weaknesses—its ambivalent feelings about the leadership of the highborn and the standards it recognized as hypocritical—than by its strengths—the exercise of a physical and economic vitality. The town was unprepared for rapid change; it did not have the security of knowing its place and its role in some overall nature of things, some tradition made permanent by the practices of generations upon generations. Bristol was not a European town fifteen-hundred years old. It was a new town that did not know what it wanted to become and lacked the leadership to find out. Bristol's condemnation of Ella at her death was based more on insecurity than on firmly held convictions about the sanctity of marriage. The twentieth century had brought change that made Bristol uncomfortable. In the nineteenth century "the trees, the war, the Negroes, [and] the river" had dominated Bristol and given it its character; then these were replaced by the movies, the automobile, and the telephone.

> These were the things which the preachers . . . railed . . . against, quoting the eschatology of Jeremiah and Isaiah and Jesus—to no effect: for the people sat in their Sunday clothes, soberly nodding agreement with all the preachers said about impending doom on earth and searing flame hereafter, and came out Monday morning as before. . . . Yet they were new to these involvements. These devices that saved labor agitated their brains, and there was an increasing dichotomy between the Business life and the Christian life; they began to have nervous stomachs. (p.181)

The new Bristol was an amalgam, a melting pot—Anglo-Saxons, Irish, Jews, Negroes, Assyrians, Chinese—but in Foote's view the pot itself had melted together with its ingredients. Overrunning and swelling are symptoms of failure. Bristol engulfed the Wingate lands; Ella swelled with an eighteen-pound fetus. Mrs. Lowry was prevented from chasing after her husband when he ran away to Texas because her legs swelled; in 1910 the president of the country was a fat man; Esther at the seminary in New Orleans spoke of Bristol with a "glut of useless knowledge"; Hector returned from Charlottesville a "plump" young man. The list could go on, but Foote's point is clear.

Glut, swelling, boundless growth for modern Bristol have no purpose and no direction.

Early twentieth-century Bristol was, according to Foote, the result of the clash and merger of two historical forces—one propelled by an agrarian ideal, the other formed by bourgeois, middle-class notions. The clash and merger were not brought about over a long period of time; the forces of history in the Delta were not the results of years of development in that place. They were forces which were imported into what was really a new land. Foote has said that he attended the funeral of the grandson of the first white man to see Lake Washington, called Lake Jordan in his fiction.[4] Washington County-Jordan County is an area which obviously never had an ancient aristocracy; there are no famous families of the Mississippi Delta as there may be of Virginia, but there were those, like the Sturgises and Wingates, who pretended to be. Juxtaposed against these people is the town that would have been better off without them.

NOTES

[1]"History as Mores: Walker Percy's *Lancelot*," *Georgia Review*, 31 (Winger 1977), 875–76.

[2]*Jordan County: A Landscape in Narrative* (New York: Dial Press, 1954), pp. 75–224. Citations are to this edition.

[3]*Stonewall Jackson: The Good Soldier* (New York: Minton, Balch & Company, 1928), p. 12.

[4]*A Climate for Genius: Transcripts of a Television Series*, ed. Robert L. Phillips, Jr. (Jackson, Miss.: Mississippi Library Commission, 1976), p. 29.

Beulah Land

NICHOLAS DAVIS

Peering down from the Vatican of a quarter century of A.I.A. journals, down the Shifting Slopes of Irreverence, across the Valley of Inverted Values, across the rubble of broken battle banners in endless ranks of ego yellow, reaction red, and media mauve, each proclaiming the irreversible finality of its truth, I can dimly see a level horizon on which there gleams the tin and timber of a tiny village, lit by the last rays of the sinking sun. And as memory draws me back into the glad green days of my youth in that village, I am struck by the amount of time and energy we architects devote to pompous polemics, and how little we really know about making places for people.

Huddling in the center of a clearing in the hardwood forest along each side of the Yellow Dog Line of the Yazoo and Mississippi Valley Railroad, the buildings wait patiently for their next train. A gravel road meanders in from Yazoo City, pauses, and loops through the village before making its way toward Belzoni. Trailing plumes of dust, tractors and trucks are coming in from fields of knee-high midsummer cotton. The cotton is stunted and drooping. There has been no rain in twenty-three days. Slowly, mules and drivers walk toward their barns in a tired tinkling of chains.

Near the depot sparrows are finishing dust baths at the edge of the road and fluttering up into silver maples to begin their roosting rituals. Bright leaves add to the frenzy, which builds in a choir of chirps, twitters, and fluttersquawks, shimmering into a pointillism of sight and sound—the evensong of every Southern town. It slowly fades with the dying light.

Someone has turned on the lights in the church. We are having our revival services every night this week. The white wooden building stands in a weedy plot on the west side of the track. It lost its steeple years ago and now has only an unconvincing lump where the symbol of fiery Methodist conviction once admonished God. It crouches there, apologizing in its weeds, with only one of its two front doors open, giving a southeast lopsidedness to its gaze. But tonight it's the brightest place in town.

The preacher arrives in his car and the crowd begins to gather on the front steps, exchanging greetings in that special church tone, shaking hands all around before going inside to sit down. The interior is completely of wood with the tired texture that comes from coats and coats of paint applied by amateurs on weekends of momentary zeal. The flat, beaded ceiling is patterned with waterstains and crossed with cracks which emit odors and particles from a sizable population of bats living in the attic.

In times past we have held impromptu bat-shoots, taking up positions outside the louvered gable ends where the bats emerge at dusk, zigzagging and twittering out into the darkening sky by the hundreds. "Here they come!" and we would rend the stillness with shotgun blasts and rifle cracks, tongues of flame squirting from our barrels, ejected shells flying about and covering the ground, spent shot rattling down on tin roofs, while the bats came and went as usual. When it was all over, the town was thoroughly annoyed and two, maybe three, little bat carcasses would lie among the empty shells, under a pale haze of gunsmoke. So, through the years, we have come to accept the bats and the kind of otherworldly presence their smell imparts to the worship service. Indeed it has become a kind of Methodist incense, pervading forever the hymns, the sermons, the stories of John Wesley.

Light comes from two bare bulbs with pull chains hanging over the aisle. Each has a swarm of gnats and moths around it, giving a vibrant flicker to the lighting effect.

"Will you play for us this evening, Miss Cassie?" asks the preacher. She always does, but never until asked. She rises, in her dignified, portly sixties, and takes her place at the piano. The preacher then, as usual, asks her to suggest a hymn. As usual, she turns slowly through the old Cokesbury Hymnal and, as always, suggests number 124,

"What a Friend We Have in Jesus," as if she were discovering it for the first time. Miss Cassie's chords are correct, but her left hand seems always ahead of her right. No one quite knows when to start singing so we wait until her voice starts, somewhere between her left and right hands. Then we join in with a slow, mournful wail that goes sliding from note to note, a shrill, siren-like wail, the women and children dominating the barely audible mumbles of the men.

"What a friend we have in Jesus,
All our sins and griefs to bear ..."

Most of the women are trying to fan and sing at the same time, adding the creak of fan handles while losing the pitch. Some have brought fancy palmetto fans, but most make do with the bent cardboard ones that say Livingston's Funeral Home on one side.

"Have we trials and temptations?
Is there trouble anywhere?"

Squirt Wigginson is sitting about three rows ahead of me with his folks. He is thirteen, like me, and his dad drives the school bus, the rumbling, wooden, 1930 International box that bumps us to school every winter. Scooter Houston is there. His folks have a plantation on Five-Mile Lake. So is Buddy McClain, whose father is the cotton gin superintendent. Squirt, Scooter, Buddy, and I are together a lot these days, and there is more to do in the village than anywhere else in the world.

We love to get our slingshots fixed up with fresh innertube rubbers, the long red kind, fill our pockets with smooth brown rocks from the road and stroll around town busting empty whiskey bottles in the weeds, splashing up geysers of water from the road ditches, and ringing the tin roofs of sheds and cotton houses.

"Watch that snuff bottle blow up when this rock hits it."

"Crappy shot! You missed it a foot. Watch this!"

"Bet I can drop a rock on Old Aunt Tamer's privy. Hope she's in there."

"There's a wasp nest in my uncle's barn big as a watermelon!"

Creaking open the wooden door we stand in the gloom till we can see the round mass of hexagons with half a hundred fiery warriors facing us and ready to sting. With our biggest rocks we stretch our rubbers to the breaking point and "One, two, three" we fire our volley. The nest explodes in chunks of splattering larvae, and a swirling swarm of red boils toward us as we dive over a low hedge and flatten in the grass like spreading adders.

"Here the sun is always shining,
Here there's naught can harm me.
I am safe forever
In Beulah Land."

Even the preacher is patting his foot to this one.

In the village there is no Little League. When we want to play ball, we round up enough kids and go to the pasture. We have no Boy Scouts with all those meetings as they have in Yazoo City. Fishing, hunting, and gigging trips are spur-of-the-moment ventures. Our summer days are not all chopped up by prearranged, organized activities, but spread out before us with the virginity of spring oat fields.

"Let's stop by Dewy Nolan's place and chew tar from his fishnets"; or we dump a bunch of tin cans off Kilby Lake Bridge and pretend they are the Japanese Navy attacking Pearl Harbor and sink the flotilla in a hail of rifle bullets. Once we caught a big spotted chicken snake and turned it loose on the Gibsons' front porch. Old lady Gibson saw it and fainted. Her husband blew a ten inch hole in the floor with his shotgun, and the snake escaped. We get carbide, seal it in molasses buckets with a little water and stand back to watch it all blow high in the air. We hunt rabbits in the cotton patches, rats in the corn cribs, and alligators in Johnson Brake. We climb on top of the gin to spy on Amy Lou Beasely taking sunbaths in her back yard.

"O, yes, I'm feasting on the manna
From a bountiful supply
For I am dwelling in Beulah Land . . ."

There is no air conditioning—the village is a big screened porch with creaky swings and cane-backed rockers. Doors and windows are opened day and night, letting in the breezes along with the sights, sounds, and smells from all around.

My bedroom window opens to the south toward several square

miles of pinoak ridges and cypress swamps, including Johnson Brake, a deep mysterious waterjungle of tangled thickets and alligator holes. On moonlight nights I lie awake and see arms of the oldest cypresses reaching into the stars above the tops of all the other trees. Watery air drifts across the palmetto ridge. I hear frog songs ranging from the shrill peepings to the deep rumblings of the bulls, rumblings that seem to gush up from the earth through amber waters and tangled roots, echoing in the belled caverns of cypress boles. The songs drift with me into deepest sleep, becoming dreams of magical rhythms keeping watch over the warm and watery darkness. And in the dew-drenched dawn, when the songs have worn themselves down to a soft drowsy murmur, I feel that I am returning from a distant land of wonders woven from the moon and the cypresses and the singing.

Each house in the village is a family portrait—people you know, rooms you know, gables that say "Hines," "Jordan," or "Denman." Windows with curtains and flowers become faces you've known all your life. Inside there are openness, as room flows into room through wide-swung doors, and the ease of aftersupper conversation in swings and rockers.

"The moon flower vines have almost reached the roof."
"Yes. Some of the buds should open tonight."
"There would be more if we could get some rain."

The houses all sit up on wood or brick piers, making a cool, dry world underneath, a twilight kingdom of heavy joists and massive piers, haunted by toads and spiders hiding in the shadows of hands-and-knees passages. Chickens cooling in dust pockets peck and scream if you tease them. Ant lions make perfect little cones in the powdery dust to trap the insect traveller that falls in. You can trick one with a broom straw, pulling it out from its cruel pit to see its hairy pinchers and then watch it go build another one, like a tiny volcano erupting. When younger we made our own dust pockets with road-ways, castles, and towns in the cool earth under the joists, unseen by people passing along the road, or walking on the floor above.

"I will sing you a song
Of that beautiful land,
The faraway home of the soul . . ."

You could hear Miss Molly sing out on this one, and bounce a little to her favorite hymn.

Miss Molly is our postmistress. The post office is in a front corner of Hines General Store, across the track beyond the depot. Every morning and every afternoon the buildings seem to lean inward to peer down the rusty rails and hand-axed cypress crossties, to hear first the hollow roar, then the whistle echoing through a mile of hardwood waterforest. Miss Molly gives the weathered canvas mail sack to Sam, the store porter, and he walks importantly to the edge of the track by the depot and waits. Steam-drenched and smoke-blackened, the little engine bursts from the trees, careening drunkenly on its uneven rails in a bell-ringing smoky celebration of the whole event.

The village pauses, waves at the engineer, helps him apply brakes, ring bells, pull levers. We watch to see whether passengers get on or off, whether the mail sack is bulging with something for us, and read the logos on the assortment of boxcars, tank cars, and flat cars with their cotton, oil, lumber—sometimes tanks, artillery, and troops. Like spectators at a horserace we strain with the engine to get its load rolling again and relax only when it disappears with a goodbye whistle into the woods on the other side of town.

Miss Molly and Sam empty the mail out onto a table behind the honeycomb of glass and metal postboxes, while a crowd gathers. The war is on and boys are scattered all over Europe and the Pacific. Tight, drawn faces watch the table and the postboxes. Nervous fingers open V-Mail envelopes.

"William's coming home!"
"Bob's on some island but he can't say where!"
"Miss Molly, are you sure there's nothing from Joe? It's been weeks!"

Whatever the news, it is shared by the folks in that little space with the oily, footworn floor, the drink and ice cream boxes, the oak and glass show cases of Tootsie Rolls, cheap watches, pocket knives and pigsfeet, and the sagging shelves of canned goods, gum boots and crosscut saws.

The preacher is praying now, about sin and death, baptism and redemption. For the war to end, and for our boys to return safely. I can hear someone crying. The preacher prays on—for Joe Spencer who is missing in action, for the Russells whose house burned last week, and finally a long prayer for rain, because everybody's cotton crop is stunted and dying from the drought.

All our drinking water comes from an artesian well near the gin. Years ago when the well was first drilled, the pipe broke off deep in the ground just as it reached water. Thinking this flow could be capped, the drillers sank a new shaft a few feet away, again reaching water. But in spite of attempts to close the abandoned shaft, the constant pressure from below has gnawed a water cavern that seems to come from the center of the earth. From a distance it looks like any other small weed-rimmed pond, about thirty feet across, with dragon flies and whirling beetles playing tag at the surface. But if you go to the edge and look down, you see that the banks are very steep and the water is unnaturally clear. Even though you can see far down before everything goes black, there seems to be no bottom. If you stand too close, a dark, bubbly mud like quicksand sucks at your feet.

"If I catch you near that well, you'll get a whipping you'll never forget," we hear from our parents constantly.

Once when Bobbie Junior Hamilton had been missing all day and people all over were searching, a group came to the well, looking along the edges for tracks and straining to see down into the deeps. Cliff, my uncle's hostler, walked out on a narrow plank spanning to the rusty water main rising from the center. He squatted and peered for a long moment then looked up at Bobby's father.

" 'Fo God, Mr. Hamilton, if he be down there, the Devil's got him."

Soon they were tying big fish hooks to an iron bar to make a drag. "Run up to Jordan's store and get that two hundred-foot spool of plow line." Squirt and I sprinted barefoot down the gravel road, our feet numb to the hurt.

Maybe the well wanted something in exchange for its water. I had almost fallen in once trying to save Squirt's young hound puppy, but something had pulled it down and out of sight. And a year or so later, walking home late one night after frog-gigging in Kilby Lake, I stopped by the well, attracted by a bubbling sound which stopped as I approached. Shining the carbide lamp into the water, I saw a thousand tiny points of silver just as a school of green-backed, mirror-scaled shiners zig-zagged under the surface. A brown and orange water snake, draped loosely over a branch, stared back at my light unafraid. The plank to the center looked sturdy so I moved carefully out to the pipe and looked down.

The light pierced far into the water, but I could see no bottom. If I fell in, I might sink forever. There was the flicker of the shiners again, the red-glowing eyes of a crawfish, sleeping sunfish in rainbow stripes of tinted iridescence, and leeches that looked like luminous pendants undulating against a night sky. I crouched for a closer look. A galaxy of creatures now glided back and forth, attracted to the cone of light. A cloud of jet black inch-long whiskered catfish boiled slowly from under lily pads. Flying saucer beetles did acrobatics, and elegant, slender insects tiptoed along the sloping sides like wisps of dried grass transformed into predators stalking unknown prey. The ooze bubbled unexpectedly here and there and things moved mysteriously just under the water lilies.

Through the light swam a soft-shelled turtle. A speckled leathery flapjack with big webbed feet and a long striped head tipped with a ludicrous trumpet-like snout. It disappeared into the slimy green stalactites that festooned downwards from the roots of the floating watergrass. The minnows made a sudden rush, a crawfish skittered backward, and suddenly there was a large brown head just under mine—a pointed, shark-like head, with red eyes and whiskers and slimy skin, attached to a rounded, wrinkled, serpentine body.

I made a wild stab with the gig and fell backward off the plank. The lamp went out and the darkness was total. My sense of direction was gone; I had swallowed some water and sought the surface, but I kept hitting slimy pipes that I thought were the creature's body. My boots and coat felt heavy. By chance, one of my arms broke the surface. I got my head up and struggled toward a faint outline of watergrass. My boot hit soft mud and sank in. The next step sank in deeper, and wouldn't come free. Pulling on grass stalks and lilies, I fell forward, pulled my feet out of the boots, and climbed onto firm ground.

As Squirt and I came running back, a bigger crowd ringed the well, calling to us to hurry up with the rope. Hurried hands made knots, and then we watched the drag splash into the water, the rope paying out and out until the spool was half empty. Then came the dragging back and forth.

"I've caught something," said Cliff. "Help me pull." Hand over hand forever, rope piling on rope on the board in wet coils, a low moaning sob from Bobby's mother. Eyes straining to make out an object rising—now no more than a dark shadow—then lighter, then dark again.

"It's snagged on something! Give me some slack!"

Three quick shots rang from the woods across the field to the north. Then a long shout. Then three more and another shout.

"They've found him," somebody said. We all left the well and went running down the cotton middles toward the woods, as the other search party emerged with a scratched and frightened Bobby.

"He got lost in a briar thicket!" I heard someone say.

I never saw so many people so happy. I never saw so many grown men cry.

All of a sudden I remembered the well and ran back. But as soon as I pulled on the rope I knew there was no more than the drag on the other end. I pulled it out and laid it in the grass at the edge of the well. The afternoon sun slanted into the water. I could see a long way down. There was only the school of shiners, the dragon flies, and a string of bubbles rising from far down in the darkness.

A much larger moth is circling the front light bulb now. The preacher's eyes make a couple of circles with it. He loses his place and has to shuffle through his notes. Buddy McClain looks over and winks at me and I have to work to keep from laughing.

Buddy's dad is the gin superintendent. He is a huge man with great slab-like hands that feel like steel when you shake hands with him. You'd have to be like that to run a gin.

Ginning season is almost as exciting as Christmas. The fields whiten with the cool nights of September and cotton is picked and piled high into slat-gated, wooden mule wagons until it spills out over the tops. Whole families ride their snow-mountain harvests towards the gin, the driver enthroned on the forward slope, handling the mules, his wife just behind, and children scattered further back, their black faces peering up from nests hollowed in the softness.

Hooves and iron wheels rumble across the plank bridge, into the gin yard and under the long waiting shed. The gin is a silver and russet city of tin and timber, ranges of peaks and pagodas connected by a network of pipes and wires. I live only a slingshot's distance away and like to walk over after school, into the cavernous engine room, into the crypt-like twilight where three giant cylinders of the Saint Mary's diesel engine ram back and forth in a blur. The terrifying noise has a pounding beat like the marches we play in the school band. On one side spins the giant flywheel; on the other, shiny cylindrical pulley-wheels turn broad black and red drive belts, slanting upward from rich, oily smells, galloping and twisting up through zigzag, oil-stained trusses and planking.

From a corner a narrow wooden stair angles up to slivers of light surrounding a door. Climbing the stair, parallel to the drive belt, one can look back down into the terrible darkness before going into the bright light of the main gin room. This space is a humming, rattling, thumping Piranesi volume with giant machines in long rows filled with razor sharp circular saws separating seed from cotton as it cascades down in white avalanches. The heavy beat of the engine is counterpointed by the multiple rhythms of complex machines. Belts turning pulleys turning shafts turning fans: sheet metal dinosaurs rearing overhead, necks and tails coiling endlessly among the rafters.

Rough wooden ladders with worn rungs scale the walls to intersect with plank catwalks high overhead. Here and there chains and knotted ropes hang from levers and switches, out of sight in the upper layers of the giant mechanism. The air is filled with the smell of cotton dust, which shines in the sunstreaks flashing down from windows high in the lint-festooned roosts of sparrows and pigeons.

Mr. McClain on the opposite side of the gin room, in an office with windows out onto the weighing platform, weighs each wagonload of cotton as it comes into position. Another man climbs onto the load and with a metal sucker pipe sucks the cotton out of the wagons up into the hollow, humming bowels of the dinosaurs.

Seeds rattle like buckshot in big metal pipes that blow them into storage buildings. The cotton is cleaned, dried, and piped to the press, where a big rotary wooden paddle tumbles it into the heavy timber pressing chamber between crushing downward strokes of a plunger. Two men work the press. When the bale is in the chamber, they rotate a big turntable, opening an empty chamber ready to receive the next bale, setting the ginned bale over the hydraulic press. The whole turntable heaves as the press starts up, compressing a fifteen-foot column of cotton into a bale four feet deep. The massive timber side-gates clang down, ties are buckled around the bale over burlap bagging, and the press relaxes. There, swelling out against its bagging and its shiny blue steel ties is the finished bale—five hundred pounds of sun and sweat and backache begun half a year earlier now lying in splendor on the timber altar in the chancel of the tin cathedral, praised by the harmonies and rhythms of the singing engines and by the proud faces of the family who stayed to watch before returning to their wagon. Even the mules celebrate by breaking into a trot, clattering the empty wagon out of the yard and over the bridge with children waving and grinning through swaying slats.

The preacher is saying something about Adam and Eve and the Serpent. I'm in the middle of a sketch of the gin on the back of an offering envelope. I hear a shriek and see several people ducking down. Miss Cassie covers her head with a hymn book and a Funeral Parlor fan; then a large bat does a loop around the front light bulb and heads straight for the preacher. He disappears behind the pulpit while the bat navigates around the edges of the little half-octagonal space where the choir would have sat if we'd had one. Then it heads straight for the front row, who divide and scatter and are quickly followed by the second row. The preacher reappears and yells to keep calm. The bat appears to be enjoying itself. With deliberate runs at people's faces, veering off at the last second, it leaves its victims stumbling backward and flailing wildly with hands, fans, and hymn books. It has a definite preference for women with long hair, as though it senses their horror of entanglement with a grotesque, unnatural fabrication of rat, bird, and pig, which hangs upside down in dark places, defecating in its sleep.

Buddy takes a swing with a broom he's found somewhere. The bat is blown off course and flies into the drop cord of the rear light, which jerks and swings back and forth, casting drunken shadows on the walls and floor. The room sways and lurches. Hymn books and old Sunday School quarterlies are thrown through the air.

The preacher has a long, limber strip of cornice molding, fallen months ago from the church eave, which he brandishes in the reeling shadows like a circus juggler. There is a thump and the bat flutters down onto the aisle floor and disappears under an avalanche of hymn books.

Feeling a bit sheepish, we pick up the clutter and dispose of the bat. The preacher suggests we sing a closing hymn, my mother's favorite.

"If I have wounded any soul today,
If I have caused one foot to go astray,
If I have walked in my own willful way
Dear Lord, Forgive."

A hasty benediction and a round of "goodnights" conclude our meeting, and we walk out under a starry sky in hot dry air, following the white of the dusty road home. A toad hops out of our path into the weeds. The rhythms of night insects seem oppressive in the heat. Frogs from the well add a slower song in a minor key, and from Johnson Brake comes the scream of an owl.

"No breeze again tonight," says my mother.

"Can I sleep out on the porch?" asks my sister.

A faint flicker lights the western horizon and we all turn to look, counting the seconds before the rumble.

"Ten miles," says my father, "and in the right direction."

We sit on our porch in the dark, as we have done so many nights this summer, and watch the sky and hope. Lightning plays back and forth along the horizon, silhouetting gaunt limbs of cypress. Billowing thunderheads glow and throb from within, like luminous creatures from the deep undersea, in puffs of pink, white, and orange.

The town holds its parched breath, not daring to believe after so many disappointments that a drop will fall. But the stars disappear under a dark eyelid, rived by a blinding network of fire that whitens the town and blinks out the lighted windows. Thunder shakes the ground in sudden blasts, and we know Father is thinking about artillery barrages he outlived in France in World War I.

A sudden watery breeze ripples the silver maples and drives hot stale air from the house through thin curtains sucked tight against bulging window screens. Between thunder crashes there comes a hollow roar.

"The rain's hit Johnson Brake," I say, recognizing the sound.

The roar grows louder and we huddle closer, shivering a bit, as we stare toward it. The pitch changes as the rain suddenly appears, breaking out of the woods into the cotton field. We can see it now, in rapid flashes, marching in white waves across the field. The first drops hit the roof of Denman's barn. Then the barn is engulfed in deep folds of a glistening garment, white like the robes of a giant ghost. The church disappears in a coiling swirl; the post office, the general stores, houses, and sheds dissolve in streaming skeins. The tall cottonwood trees in Squirt's front yard rattle, then drown. The tin seed houses ring in a rising crescendo and the gin roof disappears in a deafening crash.

We are drenched as cold drops pierce the screen and pummel the roof overhead. Solid sheets of water fall from the eaves, and we run out into the splashing, dancing whiteness. We open our mouths to the rain and take deep breaths of the new air.

And thus for a time, in that Mississippi Delta village, there was a perfect blend of man-places and nature-places, a rich variety of industry, commerce, agriculture, and residence. There were the intimate smallness and the blessed freedom needed for the imagination of a child to flourish, to bring all together in a chord which, for the architect, rings with the timeless truth of the chisels of Chartres.

Notes on Contributors

ARNOLD J. AHO is an architectural teacher and practitioner with a special interest in passive environmental systems. His *Scratchbook*, a guide for designing with natural energies, is soon to be published.

JAMES F. BARKER is an architect and educator who has a long standing interest in small towns. His focus is small town design methodology, and he has lectured and published extensively in this area. His publications include *The Small Town as an Art Object*.

EDWARD J. BLAKELY, a consultant for several international agencies on problems of economic and social development, is the author of several books, articles and monographs, including *Toward a Theory of Training People for the War on Poverty*. He is currently Assistant Vice-President, Academic Personnel Systemwide, at the University of California, Berkeley.

TED K. BRADSHAW, research sociologist and editor of *California Data Brief* at the Institute of Governmental Studies, University of California, Berkeley, has written articles and papers on California's economic development, educational system, governmental agencies, changing energy institutions and policy issues.

MICHAEL J. BUONO, associate professor of architecture at Mississippi State University, is a member of the American Institute of Architects and the International Solar Society. He co-edited *Synthesis I and II, Care Studies of Selected Contemporary Buildings* and is currently working on a book to be published fall 1980 on specialized methodology for small town design.

CHARLES A. CLINTON is an associate professor in the department of anthropology at Mississippi State University. Among his publications is *Local Success and Federal Failure: A Study of Community Development and Educational Change in the Rural South*.

197

ROBERT CRAYCROFT, a practicing architect, teaches architecture at Mississippi State University. He holds degrees in architecture and urban design. His publications include *Residential Reuse,* a manual for contractors in the field of urban residential renovation.

NICHOLAS DAVIS, architect and professor of architecture at Auburn University, is the son of Mississippi writers Reuben and Helen Davis. A recent project, a village church in Loachapoka, Alabama, has won state and national awards.

MICHAEL P. DEAN teaches English at the University of Mississippi. In addition to articles about Ellen Douglas, he has written studies on the work of T. S. Eliot and W. J. Cash.

MICHAEL W. FAZIO is an architect and architectural historian whose work focuses on Southern architecture and culture. His publications include landmark surveys, historical writings, and architectural theory.

ROBERT M. FORD, a professor of architecture at Mississippi State University, has been involved since 1962 with redevelopment and design of small towns in Washington, Illinois and Mississippi, as well as in the design of a number of public buildings.

JOHN W. KELLER is a professor in the Department of Regional and Community Planning at Kansas State University, Manhattan. As a community planning and design consultant he has specialized in land use studies and agricultural land use preservation.

DONLYN LYNDON is professor of architecture at the University of California, Berkeley. His architectural work, which has been published internationally, includes buildings and planning studies in California, New England, Maryland and Mississippi. The article presented is based on work conducted under a grant from the Graham Foundation for Advanced Study in the Visual Arts.

RONALD MURRAY, a practicing architect and associate professor of architecture at Mississippi State University, has been involved in the design of a wide range of buildings, most of which have been in small town settings.

ROBERT L. PHILLIPS, professor of English at Mississippi State University, is the author (with Scott C. Osborn) of *Richard Harding Davis* and the editor of *Antebellum Mississippi Stories.* He is book review editor for the *Mississippi Quarterly.*

FRED E. H. SCHROEDER is Director of the Humanities Program on the Duluth campus of the University of Minnesota. Among his published works are *Outlaw Aesthetics: Arts and the Public Mind*, *Joining the Human Race: How to Teach the Humanities* and *5000 Years of Popular Culture*.

RAY. B. WEISENBURGER is a professor of Planning in the Department of Regional and Community Planning at Kansas State University, Manhattan. His focus has been on small community redevelopment as a consultant for rural areas and small communities in the Midwest.

GERALD K. WELLS is Director of the Region III, Rehabilitation Continuing Education program, serving the states of Virginia, West Virginia, Maryland, Delaware, Pennsylvania, and the District of Columbia. He has made numerous studies of the American small town and its people as depicted in the writings of nineteenth and twentieth century American authors.